HERMINE VAN GULDENER

Rijksmuseum Amsterdam

TRANSLATED FROM THE DUTCH BY YDA OVINK
WITH 48 COLOUR ILLUSTRATIONS

KNORR & HIRTH VERLAG GMBH
D-3167 AHRBECK/HANNOVER

All rights, in particular of translation and reproduction, reserved. The firm of WILH. SCHRÖER & CO., *Seelze-Hannover was reponsible for the setting and printing,* KLEMME & BLEIMUND *in Bielefeld for the binding,* A. GÄSSLER & CO. *Ltd. of Munich for the colour blocks, and the Rijksmuseum for the colour photographs. Printed in Germany. A large volume in the series 'The Little Art Book', edited by* BERTHOLD FRICKE.

© KNORR & HIRTH VERLAG GMBH
1967, 1969, 1973 and 1976
Printed in West Germany
ISBN 3—7821—2111—2

The present Rijksmuseum was opened on 13 July, 1885. In 1862 a commission had already been appointed to develop plans for building a new museum. A competition for a design was announced, which specified that the museum had to house a historical department in addition to the various art collections. The Netherlands had regained their independence at the end of the French occupation in 1813 and the Prince of Orange had been proclaimed king. It was proposed to commemorate these events by a display of portraits and sculptures in a large hall or gallery. The building was expected to conform with and to emphasize the style of the 16th- and 17th-century masterpieces. P.J.H.Cuypers (1827–1921), who finally became the architect after a great deal of controversy, was a great admirer of Gothic art. Many people, however, especially in the North, did not consider this a representative national style. Cuypers's first design was decidedly neo-Gothic, but with the views of his patrons in mind he also provided a second design for the façade, which showed more Renaissance elements. In 1876 Cuypers was definitely appointed. As a result of his own development and his study of other museums, but mainly because of changes in the specifications, the necessity of a larger building, for instance, many alterations and improvements were introduced into the original design. Cuypers projected the galleries around two courtyards, a plan similar to that used by Jacob van Campen in the 17th century for the new Town Hall, now the Palace on the Dam. There is not much to be seen to-day of this plan. To cope with the tremendous expansion after 1945 of the Decorative-Arts Department, the existing rooms were extended by galleries erected on the site of the courtyard in the right wing, forming a building within a building, as it were. Admirable as Cuypers's architecture may be, new ideas on arrangement, hanging and lighting must be considered, while the collection of course continues to expand. As it is desirable that the important pieces in the national collection be concentrated in one point, and as it is practically impossible to extend the building on the outside, extension has been sought within its walls. The Historical Department re-opened in 1972 on the site of the second courtyard; the picture galleries will also be extended and a separate gallery will be reserved for exhibitions. Much of the interior decoration has been removed where modern demands require uninterrupted wall-space with no obtrusive ornaments. But the character of the building as a whole has remained unchanged and the façades will not be altered. The site of the museum, then on the border of a new urban development, led the city council to propose the construction of a through-way under the museum to connect the new upper middle-class residential area with the centre of the town. Cuypers was then faced with the problem of altering his originally planned monumental entrance in such a way that the central façade would retain its monumental character despite the passage. He has succeeded admirably. The heavy traffic of today, however, cannot be allowed under the museum and the through-way is now restricted to pedestrians and cyclists. There has been an enormous increase in visitors, especially since 1945, so that the entrances on either side of the through-way, which were more than adequate in 1885, hardly suffice after eighty years. But the museum authorities do what they can to satisfy the demands of the numerous visitors from all over the world. A restaurant has been installed in the Gothic hall where mediaeval sculptures and objects were once displayed. It is essential that visitors have the opportunity to rest and relax in large museums where there is so much to be seen and to be learnt.

Though the museum is chiefly renowned for its 17th-century Dutch paintings, works from other periods and other countries are not lacking. Sculpture never flourished in this country as, for example, in Italy and France. This is partly due to the absence of stone in the geological structure of the Netherlands. Still, we have an interesting sculpture collection. Wood-sculpture was practised here fairly extensively in the 15th century. Tapestry, a predominantly French art, also flourished for a short period in the 17th century in the North Netherlands. The wealth of the 17th-century burghers was manifested in the furnishing of their mansions and in costly utensils and ornaments. Silver, crystal, the famous Delft ware, a superb collection of Meissen china and Dutch 18th-century china, together with a rich collection of furniture, illustrate the domestic customs of the past. Three Dolls' Houses, which were not meant for children but for adult amusement, give an idea of the interior of a patrician house circa 1700. In 1945 several galleries were placed at the disposal of the Printroom, where at least part of the extremely rich collection of drawings and prints is shown in constantly changing exhibitions. The Department of Oriental Art, with objects from Indonesia, India, China and Japan, introduces us to a world with which the Netherlands have had economic relations in the course of centuries, but the cultural and artistic significance of which only came to be fully understood towards the end of the 19th and in the 20th century.

The history of these collections is often very complicated. Political and economic circumstances, the far- or shortsighted policy of curators or of benefactors who bequeath their collections, the changing fashion in taste, the increasing technical and historical knowledge of art objects, all these factors determine the character of public collections. Many people seem born collectors. Data on collections, however, seldom cover more than a few centuries. We know that people collected quite extensively in the Netherlands in the 18th century, also the Stadtholder Prince William V. In the French Revolution a part of his collection was removed to the Louvre and it was only returned to the Netherlands after much negotiation years later. Many objects still remained, however, in the various palaces and other official buildings, that seemed worth while preserving and exhibiting. In 1800 the first museum, the 'Nationale Konst-gallerij', was opened to the public in 'Huis ten Bosch' Palace in The Hague. It was later transferred to the 'Buitenhof', the former residence of the Stadtholder. Louis Bonaparte, who had been made king of Holland by his brother in 1806, was very interested in the visual arts. Amsterdam, the largest city of the country, had become the capital. The Stadtholders had always resided in The Hague, today still the traditional seat of the government. Louis Bonaparte wished to make Amsterdam the cultural centre as well, and the museum was transferred to the new capital where it was established in the Town Hall on the Dam, that had been adapted as palace in 1808. The city owned many paintings deriving from the former guilds and contributed several of these to the new museum. Among them were two of the most famous masterpieces of the present Rijksmuseum, Rembrandt's 'Militia Company' known as 'The Night Watch' and 'The Staalmeesters'. The collection was enlarged by several purchases, also of contemporary art. With the abdication of Louis Bonaparte, who had taken a keen interest in the museum, and the annexation of Holland by France, the first palmy period of the museum came to an end.

The following years reflect to a certain extent the prevailing political and economic troubles – conditions which are never favourable to the growth of cultural institutions. The museum collection was removed to a former patrician mansion, the so-called 'Trippenhuis', now the headquarters of the Royal Academy of Science, where it remained until 1885.

The history and growth of a collection is partly influenced by the current taste. The image of the museum today is naturally quite different from that at the opening in 1885. On the surface a museum may appear calm and static, but those who have the privilege to penetrate further than the public galleries are soon convinced that a museum is a dynamic 'concern'.

In the Rijksmuseum the emphasis naturally lies on the collection and conservation of art from the past. We try to demonstrate, however, by modern means that in their constantly changing formal expressions, which were determined by the spirit of a period and by differences in circumstances, the artists were essentially in touch with elements which are always fascinating.

The few surviving works of this artist who died prematurely are still completely mediaeval in presentation. His approach was hardly modern, at least when we realize that he was slightly younger than Leonardo da Vinci and a little older than Dürer. These artists, however, lived in countries with a long cultural tradition. Geertgen is one of the first artists in the North Netherlands known to us by name. Several others who later became famous, such as Claus Sluter, Dirc Bouts and Hugo van der Goes, were born in the North but migrated to Flanders where they had more opportunity for commissions. The geographical situation of the North Netherlands – a delta area of large rivers – retarded the development of the country. In comparison with France, Italy, Flanders, and Germany, this region was still in a state of evolution in the 15th century. It was hardly to be expected therefore that a young artist would be involved in the new currents which emanated from a totally different intellectual background. And yet this 'Adoration' is a work with a distinctive signature. It is known that Geertgen was a nature lover. The landscape in the background, where true to convention the arrival of the kings is situated, may be rather artificial, but the partially overgrown moat and its bank are extremely well observed. The birds on the wall also reveal Geertgen's delight in nature. Following the practice of several centuries, the men are not represented as the magi of the Gospel but as kings, one of whom had come to be represented as a black man in the course of the 15th century. Negroes had always been known in the countries around the Mediterranean, but it was only when a more intellectual approach of the world was consciously cultivated that greater attention was paid to the alien type. The three kings were obviously intended to symbolize the three continents then known and the three age groups. Though the Holy Land had become familiar through the crusades, no attempt was made to suggest an oriental atmosphere. The concept of wealth and power bowing down before the poor Child was what was important. The seated Virgin is too large but this emphasizes her central rôle. The arches of the ruins and the small water-gate stress the accent on the Holy Family. The textural treatment and the tonal values clearly show that Geertgen was a refined master of colour.

1. GEERTGEN TOT SINT JANS
presumably Leiden 1460/65–1488/93 Haarlem.

THE ADORATION OF THE KINGS
panel 90 by 70 cm. Purchased W.Hekking Junior Sale, Amsterdam, 1904.

Life and death have been curiously juxtaposed in this picture by an anonymous artist. This work must have been commissioned by the four Augustinian monks; though lacking psychological emphasis, these are unmistakably portraits. Behind them stand their patron saints, Jerome and Augustine, as they kneel by an open grave which bears an inscription:

"*Si quis eris qui transieris hac respice plora*
Sum quod eris
quod es ipse fui
pro me precor ora"
(If you should pass here, look on and weep. I am what you will be, what you are I have been. I beseech you, pray for me).

In the late 15th and early 16th century, a period of violent evolution in the Western world when man's concept of divine and cosmic dependence was being ousted by a growing self-consciousness, the threat of death the destroyer constantly appeared as a warning. Even in the life of Christ physical suffering was stressed rather than the victory of mind over matter. It is rather strange that the artist, for all his emphasis on the vanity of earthly life, should have suggested the glory of heaven by a monastery garden in which the Christ Child is riding a hobby-horse and angels are making music.

The spatial expression in the pale blue sky above the wall and beyond the gate suggests that the monastery is situated on a high point. The Virgin Mary and Elizabeth are seated on a banked mound of turf. It is very unusual for the Visitation to be represented with seated figures. The artist has very subtly expressed the character of the elderly Elizabeth in her heavy robe and veiled head, with her staff beside her as if she has just eased down her stiff joints, and in her attitude of reverential awe toward the young Virgin. Sharp angles in the Virgin's veil lend her an air of tension. The horizontal and vertical lines of the buildings and the mound stress the severity and tranquillity of the composition. Straight lines also dominate in the robes of the six foreground figures, though curves and diagonals have been introduced to relieve their comparative passivity. This is also accomplished by the asymmetrical placing. The attention is focussed beyond their heads on the Virgin and Elizabeth, and paradise. The carefully thought out composition and the refined execution indicate a mature artist who must have produced more than just this one painting.

2. MASTER OF SPES NOSTRA
thus called by G.J.Hoogewerff after this picture. Worked at the end of the 15th century, probably in Delft.

ALLEGORY ON THE VANITY
OF HUMAN LIFE
panel of oak, 88 × 104,5 cm. Probably from the former monastery Sion of the Augustines near Delft. Acquired with the mediation of the 'Vereeniging Rembrandt' in Paris, 1907.

This rather coquettish and elegantly clad woman, seated at the foot of a tree, does not immediately raise associations with a religious subject. Only familiarity with the conventions enables us to recognize her as Mary Magdalene who, especially in the 15th and 16th century, was portrayed as an extremely graceful woman with an elegant unguentarium in her hand or beside her. Scorel, who lived in Haarlem in or about 1527, was probably commissioned by the Knights Hospitallers of S. John, for whom Geertgen had also worked, to paint this saint whom they presumably held in great reverence. In accordance with the prevailing sentiment, and influenced by what he had seen on his travels to Italy, he emphasized her beauty. In the bible story Mary Magdalene was a woman of the world, to be sure, but when she ministered to Christ she had forsaken her former life. It is characteristic of the far-reaching secularization in the church that it was possible to represent a saint with all the qualities of a life she had forsworn. An additional indication that the Magdalene is portrayed here, is the rather indistinct representation of her assumption in the background near the mountain at the left. In the 16th century when the Reformation was in progress even the clergy did not always realize the import of the lives of the saints. Scorel, himself a religious, translated his admiration of Venetian art into a personal language. The mountain landscape is no longer studio-constructed; Scorel had seen mountains. He had travelled through Germany to Venice, and from there to the Holy Land. He was then appointed comptroller of the Vatican treasures, as successor to Raphael, by Pope Adrian VI, the only Netherlander ever to fill the Holy See. These memories were still fresh when he painted the Magdalene. The combination of a figure with landscape was a new motif. No attempt was made to achieve a real unity, as that would be assigning man as an individual to a minor rôle, when as a phenomenon he stood in the centre of attention. Man is now emerging from his confined world to become the conqueror of the universe; he needs more space. This was even emphasized in our picture when a strip was later added at the top. In Scorel's concept the composition had been more confined. Though the colours of his palette are also Venetian-inspired, Scorel was no slavish imitator of Italian art.

3. JAN VAN SCOREL
Schoorl near Alkmaar 1495 – 1562 Utrecht.

MARY MAGDALENE
panel 67 by 76,5 cm., circa 1527. Town Hall of Haarlem since 1625. National Museum, The Hague, since 1808.

It is not the recognition of a familiar face that excites interest in an early portrait, but the impact of a personality. This is an effect that no artist could have achieved by confining himself to a description of the exterior qualities of face and hands. In and beyond these he must have explored the inner qualities of the mind and he must have been able to translate what he found into form, rhythm, colour, and composition. An artist will always emphasize the contrasting expressions, the dynamic and the serene, in the two sides of the face. Dirk Jacobsz. has done so in this portrait he painted c. 1531 of Pompejus Occo who was then forty-eight. He was a wealthy banker and merchant, and agent for Christian II of Denmark who stayed with him in Amsterdam in 1521. He is known to have had a valuable library and to have been a very devout man, even publishing a book of prayers. Dirk Jacobsz. has not only portrayed him as a man of great dignity, but also as one who, fully aware of the transience of the earthly, has not lost faith in the eternal life. This is symbolized by the pink which Jacobsz. has at the same time used as a colour accent against the white and dark clothing. Though the deep violet, the black, and the black-flecked beige of the fur collar have been rendered in warm tones, the pointed forms on sleeves and collar are responsible for a lively note. The flowing curve of the cap is linked to the head by diagonals. The arrangement of the hands and the skull express depth, though a close analysis reveals that the man is actually standing in a rather cramped position between balustrade and wall. The impression of space is emphasized and all sense of confinement is neutralized, however, by the fantastic landscape, where a large town has been suggested in a small area, and by the sky and the white clouds. Like many other 16th-century artists, Dirk Jacobsz. has placed his subject against and not in a landscape. Pompejus Occo is evidently a very determined man, but there is no vanity in his self-consciousness. This is expressed symbolically by the skull and compositionally by the background which draws the attention away from the man into space. Composition and painting technique demonstrate that Dirk Jacobsz., the comparatively unknown son of a well-known wood-engraver and painter, is an artist who deserves more than superficial attention.

4. DIRK JACOBSZ(OON)
Amsterdam (?) before 1497–1567 Amsterdam.

POMPEJUS OCCO (1483–1537)
Banker, merchant and humanist. Was agent for Christian II of Denmark. Panel of oak, 66 × 54 cm. Purchased in New York with financial aid from the estate of Jonkheer Dr.J.Loudon, 1957.

On the old carved frame is recorded that Pieter Bicker was thirty-four years old in 1529. He had himself portrayed counting and checking his money. It is known that he was a wealthy man, that he had presumably been a brewer and had later owned a soap-boilery. He was probably a member of an advisory board of mint-masters. But who or what he had been will be of less concern to the visitor of the Rijksmuseum than the manner in which he has been portrayed as a man of dignity and action. Despite the attention given to interior and still life, this can hardly be called a genre-piece. The objects are, rather, attributes of the subject's dignity. When we trace the development of portraiture in West-European art, we see that the portrayal of the individual appeared rather late in the young culture of North-West Europe. In the representation of people many cultures attached more importance to the suggestion of general characteristics, or the indication of rank and office, than to the emphasis of the strictly personal. In the late Roman period we find many extremely individual portraits. The influence of Christianity with its strong accent on the relativity of earthly existence, however, relegated this individualism to the background. Only much later, in the Middle Ages and specifically in the 15th century, did individual characteristics again come to the fore. But the element of vanity, the ego, is not, or hardly, expressed. Man is still more or less sensible of his cosmic dependence and his predestined rôle. This feeling gradually disappeared in the Renaissance and it actually became man's endeavour to demonstrate his importance. In many portraits he fills the entire area with his presence, his head reaching to the ceiling. These compositions were not the result of faulty technique, but were expressions of the prevailing mental climate. The portraits were frequently formalized representations of the subject as a dignitary or as a scholar, an approach that had become rare in the 17th century. Pieter Bicker's pose serves to demonstrate the weight of his office. Maerten van Heemskerck has placed him slightly askance, and the still life has also been contrived so that diagonals and circular forms emphasize tension and a light action. The angular patches of light impart a three-dimensional effect to the hand that holds the book. The right hand is also skilfully handled and projects from the sleeve through a light shadow effect. Bicker's glance does not quite reflect the complete self-assurance that we find in most 17th-century sitters. The sharp lines of his face, softened by the flat round cap and the fur collar, show, however, that he was quite aware of his own powers and that he would prove himself in his work.

5. MAERTEN VAN HEEMSKERCK
Heemskerk 1498–1574 Haarlem.

PIETER BICKER
panel 84,5 by 65 cm., dated 1529.
Gift Messrs. Katz, Basel, 1948.

6. ANTHONIS MOR VAN DASHORST
called Antonio Moro,
Utrecht 1519–1575 Antwerp.

SIR THOMAS GRESHAM (1519–1579)
panel 90 by 75,5 cm. Sir Robert
Walpole Collection, Strawberry Hill;
purchased in 1779 by Catherine II of
Russia for the Hermitage in S.Peters-
burg. Acquired with aid of the 'Vereeniging Rembrandt', 1931.

When we turn from Pieter Bicker to the nearly forty years later portrait of Sir
Thomas Gresham, we are confronted by a man with a strong personality and
one who does not need the external aids of the attributes of his office. This is not
only because the subject is a totally different man, but also because of another,
more modern, approach. Moro, who was Heemskerck's junior by twenty years,
had like him visited Italy. He became a popular society painter and worked at
the court of Philip II of Spain. The court atmosphere naturally influenced his
concept of representation, but this alone did not determine his modern approach.
The 16th century was a period of far-reaching and fundamental change which
was to dominate Western thought through several centuries. The intellect and
the growing self-consciousness led men to numerous discoveries and reforms.
In the portraits of the period we constantly meet the self-assured man who
takes attention for granted. He is not, however, the type of the *bourgeois satis-
fait* that we encounter so frequently in the 17th century. There is still a measure
of reserve in the 16th-century portrait, it is not so obtrusive. In the second half
of the 16th century we see the models more freely disposed in space and their
movements have become less constrained. Sir Thomas, for example, is sitting
quite naturally and at ease in his chair. By placing gloves in the right hand, Moro
has achieved an attractive line across the pleated costume with its forward movement. In accordance with the general atmosphere of his time, in which the recording of matter was comparatively new, Moro's handling of materials, skin and
beard was extremely careful, though never fussy. It was not so much the texture
as the lively effect that was his primary concern. The folds in the two sleeves, for
example, are quite different. The entire right of the figure is, like the right side
of the face, more quiet than the left half. It is always the great artists with their
keen perception who, probably quite instinctively, stress the dual expression of
man. Moro was one of the few great North-Netherlandish artists who worked
for royalty. He had a flair for the representational that is rare in Dutch portraiture. This picture was presumably painted in Antwerp, where Sir Thomas held
the diplomatic office of financial agent for Queen Elizabeth of England. In his
letters Sir Thomas frequently reported on the growing political unrest around
1566/67 and on his discussions with men who came to play an important role in
Dutch history, among others with the Prince of Orange. This portrait therefore
has historical as well as aesthetical interest.

This is a mere fragment of what had presumably been a large work which, judging by the quality of this piece, must have been one of the finest pictures of Pieter Aertsz. Though born in Amsterdam, where he also served his apprenticeship, it was in Antwerp that he became a member of S. Luke's Guild in 1535. He married there and as he bought several houses he evidently fared well. He presumably migrated to Flanders for economic reasons like many of his predecessors. The economic and cultural growth of the North Netherlands only got under way in the second half of the 16th century, to reach its full development in the 17th century. It is quite well possible that improved conditions caused him to return to Amsterdam. Here he was commissioned to paint an altarpiece with 'The Adoration of the Shepherds' for the Nieuwe Kerk (New Church). In 1566 the altar was destroyed by the iconoclasts and only this fragment that was saved from a second disaster, the fire of the Town Hall in 1651, has survived. A fragment in Berlin (Dahlem) may be another part of the large original. Even if there had been no other work extant by Pieter Aertsz., it is evident from this picture that, in accordance with the prevailing sentiment, the religious content was essentially of less importance to the painter than his delight in men and animals that have been treated with a fair amount of realism. But this realism, which made him one of the first genre painters, was not so pronounced that he did not adhere to certain types. More than once he used a head like that of the old man with the greying hair and beard. Here he has admirably expressed the liveliness of the old man's glance as he looks over the head of the ox at the Child that was presumably lying on the ground. A second, younger, shepherd is partly leaning over him, while at the right there had presumably been a third shepherd whose staff is obliquely placed beside the head of the ox. Pieter Aertsz. was one of the first to make a portrait, as it were, of a specific animal, and he did it remarkably well. The nuances of stiff and soft hairs, moist around the mouth, the warmth and coolness of the pinkish nose with its black spots, the dark, rather suspicious, eyes, all bear witness to a true understanding of the animal, which has not just been added as a conventional attribute. It seems safe to assume that the exceptional quality of this picture had been immediately recognized and that herein may lie the reason for its survival of the iconoclasm. This may also explain the rather curious manner in which the fragment has been cut out.

7. PIETER AERTSZ(OON)
Amsterdam 1509–1575 Amsterdam.

THE ADORATION OF THE SHEPHERDS *(fragment) panel 90 by 60 cm. Formerly in the Orphan Chamber of the old Town Hall. Lent by the City of Amsterdam, 1885.*

A conspicuous feature of 17th-century Dutch landscape art is a predilection for the most static periods of nature, late summer and winter. Avercamp presumably knew the winter scenes which had made Pieter Bruegel the Elder famous in Flanders around 1560/1568. His figures which appear in large numbers on or near the ice are, however, much less involved with the frosty atmosphere and with the destitution of winter than Bruegel's. Avercamp lived in a different and less tense time, and the fact that he was deaf and dumb may have made him observe the world around him with a certain inquisitiveness. He paid more attention to the human form in his rather detailed drawings than in most of his paintings. Despite a detailed narrative where a variety of attitudes and costumes are indicated, the figures are really an integral part of the landscape in this picture. And natural as the scene may appear, it is impossible to see whether this is a frozen river or flooded land. Avercamp combined several elements that he had observed in nature in his studio. We can almost say that he composed a newsreel, with which he satisfied a need similar to that catered for by the film in our time. Above all, however, he is a refined master of colour, who has skilfully suggested in this picture the endless stretch of ice with the people dissolving in a haze in the distance. The trees have nothing of the uniformity with which many painters of winter scenes silhouette bare branches against the sky; there is something alive in them, that is also due to the tonal values in the bark, as can be best observed in the pollard willow in the foreground. Rusty, grey and pinkish tones, and a touch of blue are used for the buildings which, notably in the houses in the distance, harmonize well with the white which is made up of many nuances. The impression of cheerfulness is not caused by the people but by the red tones that the painter has playfully applied all over his composition. The faces are sketchy and the movements do not express cheerfulness. The high horizon indicates that the concept of the landscape was even more important than the recording of what he could actually see from where he stood. There is a tendency toward a more perspective intellectual construction, which is not fully developed, however. That was to be done by a younger generation.

8. HENDRICK AVERCAMP
Amsterdam 1585–1634 Kampen.

LARGE WINTER SCENE
panel 77,5 by 32 cm., signed. From the C. de Clercq Collection, Amsterdam. Purchased with aid of the 'Vereeniging Rembrandt', 1897.

Seventeenth-century fashion showed a marked preference for dignified black, a colour that only few painters can bring to life. Only the great masters, the true colourists, know how to treat this severe and sombre colour so that we do not notice its inherent lack of luminosity. Frans Hals was such a master of colour. It has been said that he used at least twenty-seven different kinds of black. The term 'colourist', however, arouses associations with bright, vivid colours. In this respect Frans Hals also proved his mastery. In the Rijksmuseum the luminous palette of Hals is especially demonstrated in the ensign in an unfinished *corps-de-garde* picture and in 'The Merry Toper'. In his uncommissioned work, where his models were mainly fisher-children and folk types, Hals was essentially the portrait painter that accorded primary importance to the individual; the social status of his subject simply did not interest him. For this reason most of Hals's pictures bear comparison very well with official portraits by other ranking artists. The name of this picture is an old, but not a very fortunate one. On closer examination, the mirth of the subject seems rather relative; the slightly parted lips do not express a generous laugh. The handling shows a richness of tone in the head and a liberal use of green in the shadows, such as we also find in Byzantine art and in many 20th-century expressionist works. Hair and beard are painted with an extremely free stroke. The raised hand with the oblique line of the white cuff gives a fine spatial effect. The hand is not stretched out toward the spectator, on the contrary, it seems to be warding him off. Hals is very 'impressionistic' here in his use of colour and in his light and shade effects. He must have influenced Manet with this kind of work. The flashy hat and the fingers curved around the stem of the glass serve to situate the man excellently in three-dimensional space. The delicate, light collar is contrived with small, rapid strokes. The supposition has been made that the medal bears the portrait of Prince Maurice. Hals probably only had a bright colour effect in mind, and chose the oval form to counteract the squatness of the figure induced by the belt. The purple cord below the medal is a sophisticated and whimsical effect that can hardly be anything but that. Hals may be mainly renowned for his superb portraits, but as a master of colour he displays an unconscious tendency toward the abstract, which is anticipatory of the more consciously handled abstract art of the 20th century.

9. FRANS HALS
Antwerp circa 1580–1666 Haarlem.

THE MERRY TOPER
canvas 81 by 66,5 cm., signed, circa 1628/30. Baroness van Leyden Sale, Warmond, 1816.

An exhibition of the work of Frans Hals, predominantly showing people who played little or no rôle in history, always draws considerable attention, and the reason for this undoubtedly lies in the attitude of mind with which Hals approached his models. Like Rembrandt he is an excellent psychologist, though some consider him less penetrating. Rembrandt's mind is strongly analytical; he wants to know and to understand. Hals frequently seems keenly direct and extrovert. In his later years his technique was indeed so spontaneous that he has often been called an 'impressionist'. The delicate collar in this picture, in which experts can recognize the pattern of the lace, is composed of daubs of white and grey, with black points suggesting openness. An enlarged detail of this collar would almost produce a 'tachystic' painting. The two white points on the left shoulder add to the airy effect. Hals uses quite a lot of grey in his white, here too in the collar and also in the white cuff, which stands away from black sleeve through the effect of a few triangles and not through a careful painting technique. The pose suggests a momentary impression. We repeatedly see that 17th-century painters create the impression of someone sitting in a three-dimensional space that is not explicitly indicated by moving the elbow forward. It is true that Hals used this device to suggest depth, but at the same time it seems to convey a certain reticence, a defensive attitude towards the outside world. If we examine the portraits carefully, paying special attention to the pose of arms and hands, we realize that the spontaneity of both Hals and his models is illusory. The attitudes repeatedly express reserve and a more or less marked defensiveness. His keen perception also inspired him to emphasize the physical difference in the two sides of the face and the attendant dualistic expression. Hals was probably deeply aware of the fact that in his *Einmaligkeit* each person must to a certain extent remain a closed book to the other. In this respect he was far ahead of his time in which knowledge stood in the centre of attention; in this respect too he is extremely 'modern' and exciting. Despite his accurate, incisive, and sometimes mocking characterization of people, they still maintain a reserve and therefore frequently acquire a certain dignity. This approach puts Hals in between 'impressionism' and 'expressionism'. It may interest the local and family historian or the art historian to know who had been his patrons, but the real fascination of Hals lies in the brillant art of his painting with which he suggests the mystery of man.

10. FRANS HALS
Antwerp circa 1580–1666 Haarlem.

NICOLAES HASSELAER
canvas 79,5 by 66,5 cm. circa 1627.
Gift of Jonkheer J.S.R. van de Poll,
Arnhem, 1885.

We do not immediately associate 17th-century still-life painting with the name of Frans Hals. Several still-life painters living in Haarlem, however, had decidedly been influenced by his handling of objects in his guard-room banquet scenes. The broad brushwork of Hals – light sparkling in glass, imparting a glow to pewter, transforming simple things into priceless objects – still arouses admiration. The object as such has become a mere pretext for constructing a composition where form, rhythm, colour and light are dominant. Compositions like these, which emphasize the still – often invisible – life, were very popular in the North Netherlands. It is related in a way to the bourgeois culture that had no need for monumental and decorative expressions of everyday life. Love of the home, of a well-kept interior, is influenced, moreover, by climatic conditions. In the first half of the 17th century simple objects predominate in still-life pictures. Pieter Claesz., for example, painted this picture in 1647 with pewter utensils, a goblet, a roll of bread, a fried fish, a lemon, a bunch of grapes and a vinespray arranged on a table that is partly covered by a white cloth. We immediately notice the broad brushwork and the extremely modern, but obviously Hals-inspired, treatment of the lemon segments. A few diagonal strokes and stipples seem to suggest its sourness, at least when we compare this lemon with the juicy ripeness suggested by Willem Kalf. The roll, the greasy fish and the bossed glass reveal an almost 'impressionist' treatment that is also noticeable in the tablecloth. But unlike the impressionists of the 19th century, Claesz. has not dissolved the palpable substance of the objects in a play of colour. This is best illustrated by the goblet which seems to reflect a window but which, despite the play of light in the liquid, still displays a remarkable solidity. The knife lying beside its case gives, together with the nutshells and the shadow of the large dish, a suggestion of depth. The spray of vine frees the still life from the matt-grey background. The arrangement of the objects on the table is of less concern to the painter than the interplay of curves and lights.

11. PIETER CLAESZ.
Burgsteinfurt (Westphalia)
1597/98–1660 Haarlem.

STILL LIFE
panel 64 by 82 cm., signed, dated 1647.
Purchased from H. Bos, Groningen,
1900.

Many artists were occupied with landscapes in the 17th century. Their drawings were probably frequently executed directly from nature; in their etchings and paintings this was seldom the case. A combination of fantasy and reality often resulted in fascinating compositions. Most of the known works of Hercules Seghers seem at first glance quite fantastic. Closer examination, however, reveals that he had probably observed the mountains he passed through on his travels with other eyes than most of his contemporaries and predecessors, that he sought another reality under the surface appearance. People who live in close contact with nature are profoundly aware of ever changing life. They are, consciously or unconsciously, confronted by invisible entities that affect change i.e. by the mystery of life. Seghers was fascinated by this process of mutation more than any other painter in the 17th century. In his work light never emphasizes tangibility or stability. It is all the more remarkable that as a man from the flat polders he primarily saw this elemental life in the mountains, which to most Dutch people seem hard and sturdily built structures. As a pupil of Gillis van Coninxloo, Seghers undoubtedly studied the mountain landscapes of Flemish artists, of whom Pieter Bruegel the Elder had been the most strongly influenced by the majesty of the cosmos. Seghers, who later mainly became famous for his exceptional etchings, must also have been acquainted with the German engravers and etchers such as Dürer and Altdorfer who attempted to express the grandeur of nature early in the 16th century. Perhaps we should put it down to a Dutch bias that he painted a valley with a river. In this picture a light colour and particularly a zigzag line lead the attention indirectly into the distance. The sunlight effects, sometimes no more than a point or a thin stroke, disrupt the atmospheric confinement. The red-roofed cottages, a few figures and the low, pointed trees moderate the solitude of the landscape, which at first glance seems rather gloomy and sad with its dark foreground and the lopped trees. Nowhere has Seghers stressed the inaccessibility of the scene, the rough surfaces and angular ridges of the rocks. On the contrary, the rocks are corroded by wind and weather, the earth is subject to change, the landscape is not a fixed quantity. This mutability, however, appears only to be influenced by elements above, and not by those under, the ground. Only in the 20th century does man discover that matter is energy. Seghers must have had some inkling of this; he seems, at least, to have felt it intuitively.

12. HERCULES SEGHERS
Haarlem (?) 1589/90–before or in 1638
The Hague (?).

RIVER IN A VALLEY
panel 30 by 53,5 cm., signed. From the bequest of Dr. C. Hofstede de Groot to the City of Groningen; acquired by exchange, 1931.

Saenredam's paintings give an excellent representation of churches and other buildings. Had he, however, not given more than a very accurate reproduction of what he had observed, he would not have interested us particularly. He is an able colourist and, notwithstanding his meticulous style, he brings bare walls to life with a subtle use of colour and light. He attached great value to documentary evidence. An inscription on this picture reads: "Pieter Saenredam first drew this after life in all its colours in the year 1641 and painted it in the year 1657". As the old Town Hall had been burnt down in 1651, he must have exercized his imagination to some extent to achieve such a wide range in the colour of the buildings. This picture hung in the Burgomasters' office until 1940. In 1648 it was decided to build a new Town Hall that would be more befitting to the importance of the town, which was for a short time in the 17th century the largest port in West Europe. The old Town Hall, with the Burgomasters' chamber in the tower, had become much too small and had fallen into decay. Grass sprouted between the stones and the walls were crumbling. In fluent tones of yellowish white and grey Saenredam contrasted its weather-worn aspect with the white plastered surface of the neighbouring house. This house, too, is not new. The faded buff shutters and the grey timbers below create a rather weary impression. The red in the tower, a small dark-red spot in the skirt of the seated woman, a touch of red on the shutter of the partly visible pinky-hued house at the left, these are bright tones that, together with diagonal and curved lines, animate the scene. The roofs and spire are sharply silhouetted against the blue, lightly cloudy sky. The houses which are only just indicated at the left and the right serve less to mark the limits of the composition than to suggest a street that continues in both directions. The curious grey object hanging by a chain on the wall is a whalebone, a reminiscence of whaling expeditions and trade. For Saenredam, however, it represents a beautiful broad, grey line that helps to guide the eye round the corner. This picture is significant for the history of Amsterdam, but as a work of art it equally merits attention, and it provides a fascinating comparison with Vermeer and later painters of town scenes.

13. PIETER SAENREDAM
Assendelft 1597–1665 Haarlem.

OLD TOWN HALL OF AMSTERDAM
panel 64,5 by 83 cm., signed. The painting was bought by Burgomasters of Amsterdam on 30 July, 1658 for 400 guilders, to be hung in the Burgomasters' Chamber. Lent by the City of Amsterdam.

Though his early work was richly animated with figures, Jan van Goyen is primarily a painter of landscapes. In his drawings we also notice a preoccupation with bustling activity, but less as individual action than as a general impression, usually in relation to a landscape. In this large picture the three figures merely serve as agents to lead our glance to the distance by their position on the ridge. Here the two ancient trees against the vast expanse of the grey sky are the protagonists. This picture is exceptional in the development of landscape art because here, more than in any other contemporary work, we are aware that the trees are growing out of the earth and that rotting is a process of internal decay. This is evident when we compare these trees with those painted by other artists, where we frequently get the impression that the trees have been set down on the surface; despite an accurate observation of the peculiarities of bark and foliage, the observation in itself has not seldom remained the chief concern. It is of course quite understandable that 17th-century artists attached primary importance to the recording of objects at a time when the intellect, the curiosity about everything that was perceptible, dominated the relatively new culture of Western Europe. There would, however, be no question of art if an awareness of what lies under the surface appearance is lacking. Van Goyen emphasized these invisible, but none the less perceptible, elements so strongly in some of his paintings and drawings that they almost strike us as modern. In this picture the leaves have been mainly rendered by small, greyish brown touches which are quite distinct from the branches; but Van Goyen has also applied practically triangular, light-green daubs in the foliage so that a certain tension is involuntarily transmitted. This was probably quite unintentional. Van Goyen seems to have been fascinated in these trees by the crumbling decay in which a spark of life still lingered on. It seems logical, therefore, that he instinctively made use of free brush-strokes, forms, and lines that convey tension. These bare, gnarled branches, outlined against a grey sky and a rather desolate landscape, were greatly admired by the Romantics. Today it is mainly the awareness of the life and tension in nature that arouses admiration.

14. JAN VAN GOYEN
Leiden 1596–1656 The Hague.

LANDSCAPE WITH TWO OAKS
canvas 88,5 by 110,5 cm., signed and dated 1641. L.Dupper Wz. Bequest, Dordrecht, 1870.

Judith Leyster, one of the few woman painters in the 17th century, was in no way inferior to many of her male colleagues. Many of her pictures were in fact for many years attributed to her teacher Frans Hals. Hals had many pupils, but only rarely do we find in their work a trace of the dashing *élan* that had made him famous. Judith Leyster, who worked with him in 1629, was only twenty years old when she painted this portrait. The influence of Hals is clearly perceptible in her broad handling of the brush. Judging by her use of light and the choice of motif, however, it seems very probable that she had previously been a pupil of Hendrick ter Brugghen in Utrecht, or had at least been strongly influenced by the Utrecht followers of Caravaggio. There we repeatedly find knee-length portraits of musicians, executed in a rather dashing style. Judith Leyster tried to give a personal interpretation of what she had been taught in Utrecht and Haarlem. She introduced no new elements into Dutch painting, but this early work displays a fresh outlook and a well-developed technique. The shadow effects in the head and the light that emphasizes the white around the dark eyes and of the teeth introduce a witty element. Underneath a jaunty feathered cap the light-brown hair falls down onto the shoulders. The airy collar, the pointed cuffs, the glow of the greeny yellow silk, and the red breeches edged with yellow also add to the vivid effect. Judith Leyster made an effective use of diagonals to suggest both depth and motion. Only very few artists have been able to suggest the playing of music by transmitting a musical rhythm in form, line, and colour. This problem has, as a matter of fact, only been consciously posed with the advent of cubism in the 20th century. Most artists proceed from the act of holding the instrument. Though the hands have been well observed, Judith Leyster has not suggested the lightness of the strumming; the shadow of the right hand is too heavy. The decoration of the sound-hole is executed in short strokes, but even so the lute is still a rather massive instrument. Taking everything into account, this is a remarkable picture for a young woman of twenty, and far more interesting than most of the works of Jan Miense Molenaer, the man she married in 1636, who had also been a pupil of Frans Hals.

15. JUDITH LEYSTER
Haarlem 1609–1660 Heemstede.

THE SERENADE
panel 45,5 by 35 cm., signed and dated 1629. From the Six Collection, Amsterdam, purchased with aid of the 'Vereeniging Rembrandt', 1908.

16. SALOMON VAN RUYSDAEL
*Naarden shortly after 1600–1670
Haarlem.*

RIVER SCENE WITH FERRY
*canvas 99,5 by 133,3 cm., signed and
dated 1649. From the 'Dienst voor
's Rijks Verspreide Kunstvoorwerpen',
1960.*

It is mainly in the 17th century that river scenes occur in Dutch art. At no earlier or later period did the great rivers with their boats and ferries, the latter a characteristic feature of the lowlands even in this century, form a major subject of Dutch painting. The painters of the Hague School did, indeed, quite frequently use the polders as a motif, but then the landscape is either intersected by ditches or it is marshy. It is not easy to find a demonstrable explanation for this. Landscape as such, as a scene imbued with atmosphere, makes a comparatively late appearance in Western art. In the early Middle Ages an indication of the idea sufficed. It was only when Western man began to observe the world around him intellectually that his interest in landscape was aroused. Both overseas and inland shipping is of vital importance to the economic life of the Netherlands. Many 17th-century river scenes bustle with life, and yet they lack the serious activity that indicates that the rivers were, and are, trade routes. The ferries that appear in the work of Esaias van de Velde and particularly Salomon van Ruysdael mainly serve as *repoussoir*. They help to direct the eyes to the horizon, and with the figures of men and animals they animate the scene. The surface of the usually placid water is only ruffled to suggest the reflection of trees, cows and men. Motion is suggested by diagonally placed sails and flags, though it is a moot point whether sailing would be possible at all under such still conditions. Though the artist has admittedly suggested a slight breeze here by his treatment of clouds and trees, the desire for a tranquil atmosphere seems predominant. Houses, boats, ferry, water, the bank that runs obliquely toward the horizon, everything is intensely quiet. The painter has undoubtedly observed nature well, with a keen appreciation of the light playing through the trunks of the trees and the leaves. With small touches he even suggests a slight scintillation of light. The atmospheric tranquillity and the expanse of the scene where men and animals are subdued were, however, much more important to him. The use of rather light colours, frequently with a touch of red in the dark costumes, gives a sunny and friendly impression to many of his pictures.

In comparison with his uncle Salomon, Jacob van Ruisdael's work seems rather heavy, sometimes even romantic and melancholy. But it would be wrong to call him a 'Romantic', the emotional effect is too light. He was obsessed by the problems of light – how it emphasized form and effected changes in colour. His clouds are therefore apt to be rather solid; though light plays through and around them, we are hardly reminded of their ethereal and unsubstantial quality. They cast heavy shadows on the ground that, according to a long-standing convention, is constructed in three planes. In Jacob van Ruisdael's work this construction repeatedly leads to a rather tight composition, with practically no suggestion of infinite expanse. He interprets what he has observed with more or less imaginative power, never neglecting the balance of his composition, however. Seventeenth-century landscapes often make a rather crowded impression. The rushes hanging over the water in this picture, gently swaying in the breeze, involuntarily call to mind Chinese and Japanese paintings where infinity is suggested by a single stem against a hazy background. Ruisdael surmised something of this; on the other hand, the sense of delight in all he saw was still so novel in the experience of Western man that he was hardly ripe for a philosophical attitude of mind and an awareness of the relativity of matter. And yet, matter is never the essential aim for a true artist. The mill is a very substantial object, but the painter delights above all in the light that outlines it against the sky, and in the contrast between curved forms and sharp lines. Like the other vertical forms and lines, the tower and the houses provide a stable element in contrast with the ruffled water and the ground. As human beings the three light figures are completely negligible, but as notes of colour and form they are as indispensable as the large white sail at the left. They moderate the heaviness of the landscape. The season in Ruisdael's landscapes, like in those of many of his contemporaries, is usually late summer or winter when nature seems least active. We seldom encounter growing flowers, though we know from the flower-pieces that men were not indifferent to their colourful display. The work of many 20th-century artists is based on the concept of the invisible, but always perceptible, dynamic element in nature, in the realization that matter is energy. The 17th-century artist's observation of nature was confined rather to externals. He did not, or hardly, realize that what he observed on the surface was influenced by forces below and above the earth. Even so, the approach of painters like Jacob van Ruisdael opens our eyes to otherwise unheeded beauties of landscape.

17. JACOB VAN RUISDAEL
Haarlem 1628/29–1682 probably Amsterdam.

THE MILL AT WIJK BIJ DUURSTEDE
canvas 83 by 101 cm., signed, circa 1670. Bequest to the City of Amsterdam, 1854, by A. van der Hoop, Amsterdam. On loan, 1885.

Jacob van Ruisdael had been living in Amsterdam for quite some time when he painted this view of Haarlem. The distance between the two towns, however, is not great and we can safely assume that he returned to his native town more than once. We know that he liked to travel; he visited West Germany and he must have spent a fairly long time in France as he graduated as a doctor of medicine at the University of Caen in 1676. There is not much on record concerning his scientific work and his medical practice; he is much better known as a painter and etcher of landscapes. Both his father Isaac and his uncle Salomon were painters. He was familiar with landscape painting from childhood. Haarlem, where many Flemings had settled after the outbreak of the 80-year's war with Spain, was a flourishing town at that time and many artists made a reasonable living there. The weaving and bleaching of linen were important industries as the local dune water was exceptionally suitable for linen processing. Jacob van Ruisdael was fond of wandering in the dunes and he frequently expressed his obsession with the view of Haarlem from a high vantage-point across the bleaching grounds. From one or two points we can even still enjoy this prospect; the bleaching grounds have now disappeared, but there are instead the colourful patches of the bulb-fields in spring. The horizon has been taken very low in this picture so that Ruisdael had the opportunity of painting a wide sky, with heavy clouds casting their shadows on the ground. The sun breaks through the clouds, giving more relief to the houses with S.Bavo's church towering over them. On the ramparts of the town are several windmills; Ruisdael needed the white sails with their suggestion of three-dimensional space in his scene. The long strips of linen in the meadows are also very helpful in achieving a three-dimensional effect. The red roofs at the left provide warm notes of colour in the dark landscape that forms a tight composition despite the wide view. The town is surrounded by a dense circle of green; the houses in the fields are mostly hidden in the trees. Ruisdael's handling of the sloping roofs and the pointed lines of the spires enlivens the composition considerably. Though the town and its surroundings are clearly recognizable, the whole construction of the picture indicates that it had been painted in the studio. The painter undoubtedly made his sketches from nature, but he used them as aids for his fantasy and his expression of the light-dark relation that fascinated him.

18. JACOB VAN RUISDAEL
Haarlem 1628/29–1682 probably Amsterdam.

VIEW OF HAARLEM
canvas 43 by 38 cm., signed, circa 1670. L.Dupper Bequest, Dordrecht, 1870.

Paulus Potter signed his name prominently on the stile. He had indeed cause to be proud of the fact that as a young man of twenty-four he already had a reputation as an animal painter. Here was a new motif that evidently enjoyed a great popularity and was assiduously copied. This may perhaps be related to the extensive investments in landed property and land-reclamation schemes by people who had made money in trade. Many of them acquired country estates, and in their pride of property, that may have included a breeding stud, they probably desired a portrayal of their cattle. Horses and other animals had of course appeared in pictures before this, but then mostly in scenes of men on horseback, the ox and the ass in Nativity scenes, dogs and birds in their relation to men. Potter paints the portrait of an animal. He places his cattle and horses in a meadow and tries to show them as they really are without people. He frequently suggests an atmosphere of summer. Though much of his work had presumably been commissioned, there are several other pictures with deer, goats, and dogs that also reveal Potter's great love of animals. In this picture a storm seems imminent – the sky is lowering, a wind is starting to blow, and the horses stand nervously tense. Potter has particularly tried to express this tension in the heads, the flowing manes, and the switching tails. The legs of the dark-brown horse, however, are solidly planted on the ground, with no trace of a nervous tremor. In the white horse this has been expressed more successfully The artist was still young, and though he was a painter's son and familiar with the craft from childhood, he looked about him with new eyes. At a time when substance and plastic forms were highly valued, he attempted to express the atmospheric tension where substance dissolves and becomes intangible. It was not until the 20th century that this problem was consistently tackled by Franz Marc. That Paulus Potter had even posed it is in itself remarkable. In The Hague he had been the neighbour of Jan van Goyen for a short time and it seems highly probable that he became acquainted with his ideas. In some of Van Goyen's paintings and notably in several sketches it is evident that the narrative had become subordinate to the atmosphere. Neither Potter nor Van Goyen, however, avoided the construction of the landscape in three planes. It is rather remarkable that Potter often painted flowers in the grass. These can only be seen, indeed, when we look closely, but they do add a certain liveliness to the grass, that is rendered in this picture by rather bright green stalks among which a few yellow flowers appear; this colour always has a rather dynamic effect, though that is admittedly minimal here.

19. PAULUS POTTER
Enkhuizen 1625–1654 Amsterdam.

HORSES IN A FIELD
panel 23,5 by 30 cm., signed and dated 1649. Bequest to the City of Amsterdam, 1854, by A. van der Hoop, Amsterdam. On loan, 1885.

Rembrandt frequently chose his models from his immediate environment. With the state of mind typical of the introvert, he was constantly moved to explore the same person, the same story even, from different angles. As his personal experience became greater, his ability to characterize a situation also evolved. Rembrandt portrayed his mother several times, but in this picture his interest was centred less on her personality than on the attitude of reading. Practically no other artist showed such a concern with the significance of a book as Rembrandt did. He has recorded in many compositions how people use their books – they are simply reading or they are engrossed in study, reading inspires them to thought, it enriches their mind, it also provides them with arguments. The woman here is reading quietly. Actually the heavy volume can hardly be held in this way, but the hand with its dark shadow and the dark patch across the page keep it from slipping away. The face is merely suggested. All attention is concentrated on the hand, with the emphasis on the fine wrinkles of this old, but still very lively and plastically shaped hand. Despite his attention to detail, Rembrandt did not neglect the composition as a whole. Compared with the light effect across Jeremiah's robe (cp. pl. 21), the light falls more into the folds here. Under influence of the dark red of the cloak it imparts a warm tone. The golden glow on the rather curious headdress, together with the flowing lines and the broad folds of the robe draped over the chair, intensifies the impression of mental activity. The tome is obviously not being read for the first time. The slightly diagonal attitude and the forward inclination of the body bring depth into the picture, but the spectator's attention is not riveted in the background. Notwithstanding his great concern with three-dimensional space and man's relation to it, Rembrandt nearly always – unconsciously – seeks to know: how does it feel, what is it. He seldom says: what do I see (with the accent on I), where the attention is usually concentrated on a specific point.

20. REMBRANDT HARMENSZ.
VAN RIJN
Leiden 1606–1669 Amsterdam.

REMBRANDT'S MOTHER
panel 60 by 48 cm., signed and dated 1631. Bequest, 1928, by M.P.Voûte to the 'Vereeniging Rembrandt'. Taken over, 1928.

A remarkable aspect of Dutch 17th-century art is the religious picture that was not initiated by the church. Many religions instigated the portrayal of sacred events. This became a medium for teaching the unlettered masses and inciting them to devotion. But 17th-century Holland was mainly a protestant country where altars and images were undesirable and prohibited. Rembrandt's interest in the bible derived to a large extent from his desire for a better understanding of man in all his reactions. He probably considered the stories from the bible, that were widely known then, as classic examples of human problems in the first place. As a young man Rembrandt was fascinated by old people; their faces seemed to acquire more meaning through their wrinkles. His work was still strongly influenced by the academic tradition and the recording of detail was, therefore, very important, but Rembrandt certainly did not stop there; he has animated the wrinkled head with the fine hair and the flossy beard. In the gold vessels and the wide border of the robe his love of scintillating light is already revealed. The contrast of light and dark – an extensively explored problem at that time in Western Europe – almost gives a floodlight effect here. It strongly emphasizes the plastic forms. Though it seems unlikely that Rembrandt actually had an old man pose for him in this attitude, he had studied the type well. Several drawings are known of a similar head. When we compare these with the painting, we see how in the development of the motif Rembrandt has probed deeper into the personality of the dejected old man, wrapt in thought, who is paying no attention to what is happening in the background. The glow of the vessels, the diagonal line of the arm, a few sharp folds, however, dispel all passivity from this attitude. The burning city, the soldiers in the gate-way and a few other figures are no more than a background that explains the solitary and withdrawn old man. Despite the small picture area, it is already evident in this passage that Rembrandt was – unconsciously – searching for larger forms.

21. REMBRANDT HARMENSZ. VAN RIJN
Leiden 1606–1669 Amsterdam.

JEREMIAH Lamenting the Destruction of Jerusalem
panel 58 by 46 cm., signed and dated 1630. Gift of the 'Vereeniging Rembrandt' and private citizens, 1939.

In various drawings and etchings of the thirties Rembrandt showed his concern with the problem of assembling people in action into a group. When he received a commission from the Arquebusiers' Guild, it became urgent to find a solution for this problem, which even today still puzzles film-makers and photographers. There was practically no court culture in the North Netherlands, but the patricians who founded their guilds and societies desired to be portrayed in formal group portraits; proud of their honorary office, they wished to display their consequence and that of their friends. In the 16th century the militia companies had already been portrayed with the men neatly lined up as in a 'club photo'. In the 17th century the painters tried to bring more action into the groups, but it required a self-willed man like Rembrandt, who simply ignored the vanity of his patrons, to discover the classic solution for what is quintessential in a group: "unity in diversity. No man is important by himself". The captain does indeed come to the fore here as the commander of the group, but without the lieutenant and the men he would have no significance. The group is patently approaching the spectator, but not for a moment do we get the impression that it is marching down from the wall; it is restrained by the figure of the captain. Though the men are standing close together, everyone can move freely; each is occupied in his own way and no-one draws more attention than his neighbour. Rembrandt, who was only thirty-six when he completed the picture, was here especially concerned with the psychology of the group. Fascinated as he was at the time by all the problems of the Baroque, he was interested in movement rather than in individual emotion. A complication for all painters of *corps-de-garde* pictures was that they had to consider the situation of the picture in the Guild Hall. The size of the picture, the lighting, the impression made on a visitor entering the hall, all these factors were extremely important for the composition. Rembrandt's picture was originally meant to be hung in the corner of a large hall. He undoubtedly kept this in mind. A close examination, borne out by radiographs, reveals that Rembrandt had made alterations in the composition so that it would have the liveliest effect when seen from the right. The long, mainly diagonal, lines of the weapons suggest three-dimensional space. The dynamic yellow of the lieutenant's dress is repressed by the shadow of the captain's hand. The black costume of the latter, which is enlivened by the red sash and the white collar, keeps the whole group within the framework of the composition. By a sophisticated manipulation of line, form, and colour Rembrandt has created the impression of holding a transient moment. A patron wishing to see his self-importance reflected in his portrait would decidedly not be pleased with this lively representation where the individual is completely subordinate to the group. The lack of contemporary appreciation of Rembrandt's composition is

22. REMBRANDT HARMENSZ. VAN RIJN
Leiden 1606–1669 Amsterdam.

The Militia Company, known as THE NIGHT WATCH
canvas 359 by 438 cm., signed and dated 1642. Formerly in the Major Court Martial Chamber of the old Town Hall, Amsterdam. Transferred to the 'Trippenhuis' in 1815. Lent by the City of Amsterdam, 1808.

therefore, quite understandable. The rather unfortunate name 'The Night Watch' is first recorded in the 18th century. In comparison with many contemporary *corps-de-garde* pictures this painting is relatively dark. Practically no attention was paid at the time to the virtuosity of the composition. What did draw attention was the fact that Rembrandt had represented his vain patrons as 'too ordinary'. Rembrandt wished to create the impression of a group emerging from a dark building. The unique solution of the forward movement and the unity of the group has made this composition a justly renowned picture. Yet Rembrandt was to reduce motion considerably in his later work in order to emphasize emotion.

In this panel from about 1644 a reading figure is again represented. There is no suggestion at all of letters and lines and yet the book is being read with close attention. The profile of the woman with the sharp nose, an angle in her back, and a small triangle on the book are the main elements expressing tension. Though the light across the white pages is important for the three-dimensional effect, the dark figure, behind which a light has seemingly been placed, serves to divert the attention again from the wall. The old woman, whose large, angular shadow emphasizes the height of the room, is holding a rope to rock the cradle. In the years of his marriage with Saskia van Uylenburgh Rembrandt made several drawings of children, often in the company of adults. It is also evident here that he had observed children closely. The essence of deep sleep is not only indicated by the way the baby lies, but is also stressed by the gentle modelling of the cover. Rembrandt must have seen compositions with the theme of S. Anne, the mother of the Virgin, with the Virgin and the Child, where the three figures were usually depicted rather solemnly together. But as he was not executing a church commission, and the human element intrigued him more than anything else, he developed this theme within the context of his own environment. It is highly improbable that the crouching figure, seen on the back in the foreground, was meant to be S. Joseph. The curves of this figure were necessary to fill in the dark empty space below the stairs. The composition is a rhythmical construction of vertical, horizontal, and curved lines. Many objects have been used for their form rather than for their function. The shape of the basket hanging on the wall at the left, for example, is similar to that of the neckerchief of the young woman. Rembrandt had originally painted it hanging over her head, but the effect must have been too heavy and he painted it over. This is one of the typical *pentimenti* that are so numerous in Rembrandt's pictures. The light has a spatial rather than a plastic effect. Rembrandt developed

23. REMBRANDT HARMENSZ. VAN RIJN
Leiden 1606–1669 Amsterdam.

THE HOLY FAMILY
panel 66,5 by 78 cm., fragmentary signature, circa 1644. Acquired, 1965, from the collection of A. R. Boughton Knight, Downton Castle, with aid of the 'Vereeniging Rembrandt'.

the contrasts of light and shade in various ways. This picture represents a phase that lies between the technical approach of the 'Jeremiah' picture and the mainly psychological approach in 'S.Peter's Denial'.

In this picture Rembrandt shows the psychological insight of a man who has himself been through many bitter experiences. In a drawing of a slightly earlier date he had followed the bible text quite faithfully, emphasizing the situation, whereas the inner conflict of S.Peter is now the main theme. Judging by the bewildered expression of the woman with the candle, Peter has apparently just denied her assertion that he too had surely been one of the disciples. The soldier holding the flagon is not impressed by the denial. Under cover of his cloak Peter clasps his right hand against his chest as if in fright; he shows a certain hesitation which is further stressed by the gesture of his left hand. The treatment of the hand is 'expressionistic' and the old man's head has also been conceived on generous lines. Thirty years after the 'Jeremiah' all detail has been subordinated and the bearded face has been composed with colour and light. The spectral figures of Christ and several soldiers and high priests are extremely remarkable. Unseen by Peter, Christ seems to be turning towards him as if he knows that the moment of the denial had come as he had foretold. At the left another figure is practically hidden in the shadow. It is a rather coarse-faced soldier who seems to have adopted a waiting attitude. The woman's question has made Peter realize that good and evil are still contending within him, that he is not as unequivocally good as he had thought. The question unwittingly has great significance. Rembrandt must have known from his personal experience what the consequences could be of a chance remark made by someone who was ignorant of the circumstances. He probably saw this guileless and innocent woman as an instrument of God. She is shedding the light on Peter; she is acting by intuition; she had to ask the question though she does not realize why. Rembrandt did not use the light for the plastic emphasis of her head, but as an indication of her ingenuity. The spectral forms of Christ and the soldier seem to symbolize good and evil, the elements between which Peter is now beginning to distinguish. Rembrandt has quite intuitively given a psychological analysis here. In composition, rhythm, and colour this work also represents one of the most important religious pictures ever made by him.

24. REMBRANDT HARMENSZ. VAN RIJN
Leiden 1606–1669 Amsterdam.

S. PETER'S DENIAL
canvas 154 by 169 cm., signed and dated 1660. Purchased by Catherine II of Russia for the Hermitage in S.Petersburg. Acquired with the aid of the 'Vereeniging Rembrandt', 1933.

The arrangement of hands and legs of people grouped around a table is a tricky problem even now, on the stage, for example, or on a photograph. Rembrandt had presumably studied many group portraits by his predecessors, where the hands – sometimes awkward, sometimes mere white patches – were mainly noticeable for their lack of function. Twenty years after 'The Night Watch' Rembrandt's concern was chiefly with emotion. Movement has been reduced to a minimum in this group of gentlemen gathered around the table. One hand only is shown of each and then only partially, while the hands of the servant with the black skull-cap are invisible. Yet each gesture is the interpretation of an inward reaction, and compositionally all hands are directed towards the book. Rembrandt has grasped the significance of this book in the meeting exceptionally well; it evidently contains arguments to be used in refutation of some person or proposition. This is emphasized by the gesture of the rather severe man in the centre. His severity is determined less by his facial expression than by the straight lines of his hat and the flat expanse of the collar. Like other great artists Rembrandt employed the device of indicating or animating an expression by the inherent forms of objects. The names of the sitters have been established with a fair amount of certainty, though we do not know who is who. Rembrandt fascinates us most, however, when he transcends the incidental and the individual to characterize the universal in man. This picture, too, is an instance of Rembrandt's classic solution for a group, here represented by a meeting; again we see unity in diversity. He probably reached this psychological solution quite unconsciously. Preliminary studies for this composition and radiographs demonstrate how in the course of execution Rembrandt constantly made alterations which were always improvements. In his later years Rembrandt came to realize more and more that intensity of expression is achieved by tension in form, line, and colour. The book is composed of but two small triangles and a few lines. Angles and sharp lines in the panelling are opposed to the broad expanse of the red table-cloth. Three-dimensional space is suggested by the effect of light on the wall and the white collars. Yet everything is attuned to unity and rest.

25. REMBRANDT HARMENSZ. VAN RIJN
Leiden 1606–1669 Amsterdam.

'THE STAALMEESTERS' (the Sampling Officials of the Draper's Guild) *canvas 191 by 279 cm., signed and dated 1662. Formerly in the Staalhof (Draper's Guild Hall) in the Staalstraat in Amsterdam. In the Town Hall, Amsterdam, since 1771. Lent by the City of Amsterdam 1808.*

26. REMBRANDT HARMENSZ.
VAN RIJN
Leiden 1606–1669 Amsterdam.

The Bridal Couple or
'THE JEWISH BRIDE'
canvas 121,5 by 166,5 cm., signed,
fragmentary date 16.., circa 1665.
Bequest to the City of Amsterdam, 1854,
by A. van der Hoop. On loan, 1885.

Names have been proposed to identify this couple and it has even been suggested that they may represent Isaac and Rebecca. It is not at all certain that a portrait was intended and considering the gesture, it seems very unlikely that it was a commissioned work. The handling of the heads, however, suggests that Rembrandt must have based himself on actual people. In comparison with the numerous portraits of married couples painted in the course of time, Rembrandt has, more than anyone else, touched here on the spiritual relationship and the warmth of feeling between the partners. With his instinctive psychological insight he realizes that the *Einmaligkeit* of the individual also implies a certain reserve and a certain respect for the other. In the 17th century, and even long after, many artists emphasized the dignity or the felicity, frequently with an element of sensuality, of the married couple they were portraying. Despite the distressing circumstances in his life, Rembrandt always maintained a positive mental attitude. His late work bears witness to a wise understanding and to an awareness of the relativity of all matter. In his painting this led him to an ever greater reduction of textural representation. In this picture the style of dress is not recognizable. The emphasis in the costumes is on the warm, deep red that is enlivened by flecks of yellow. The man, who is gently drawing the woman towards him, has a luminous yellow, broadly moulded sleeve. The dynamic yellow, however, is restrained by dark tones. The hesitancy of the woman, who is apparently still sunk in reverie, is mainly suggested by the angular lines of the skirt and by the broad diagonal which has been constructed with the palette knife in an opposing movement. The jewellery has been added for its sparkling effect. The treatment of the hands is an extremely subtle, quiet composition of lines. In his painting technique and handling of colour Rembrandt is quite 'expressionist' here.

The Portuguese synagogue in Amsterdam was built in 1674/75 by Elias Bouman. This sober and severe edifice, encircled by low houses, is still one of the most interesting landmarks of the city. Though its immediate environment was considerably altered in and after the last war, the memory of the Portuguese refugees who played such an important rôle in the economic and cultural life of the 16th and the 17th century is still alive here. Emanuel de Witte may have been commissioned by a member of the Portuguese community to depict the rather large new synagogue. This sort of thing must have occurred regularly, though conclusive evidence is usually lacking. We should bear in mind, however, that people often expected no more of a painter than we do of a modern press-photographer. Emanuel de Witte specialized in the painting of interiors, often of churches. He made a thorough study of the problems of perspective, but he is at the same time too good an artist to conform strictly to the mathematical order. He was even more absorbed by the problem of creating a three-dimensional effect by the use of light and shade and colour, often paying more attention to the compositional effect than to an accurate recording. The lofty building with its many windows and long lines has been treated with great accuracy here. In his treatment of the congregation, however, De Witte is not concerned with individuals but with colour and spatial effects. The figure seen on the back in the long pale-blue cloak with red facings acts as a *repoussoir*, a device used more than once by De Witte. The woman in the white kerchief is making an expressive gesture, but it is obvious that De Witte needed it as a counter-movement. The bronze ornaments enliven the dark oak panelling and the large bronze chandeliers which are still in use today relieve the linear severity with their glowing, curved arms. Though the windows have been painted rather opaquely so that they restrict rather than aid the view, De Witte has flooded the walls and pillars with sunlight. The long red curtains and the light figure in the foreground form a positive and vivid colour effect. Despite the presence of many people, children, and even dogs, the atmosphere would have been subdued and gloomy without these light tones.

27. EMANUEL DE WITTE
Alkmaar circa 1617–1692 Amsterdam.

THE PORTUGUESE SYNAGOGUE
in Amsterdam
canvas 110 by 98 cm. Formerly in the Kaiser-Friedrich-Museum, Berlin. Purchased from Messrs. Duits, London, 1949.

The work of Willem Kalf forms a great contrast with that of the twenty years older Pieter Claesz. This should not only be ascribed to a difference in personality, but also to the influence of a younger generation of buyers with more expensive tastes. Around the middle and in the third quarter of the 17th century there was a general tendency toward luxurious living. Though we recognize an appreciation of fine silver and china in Kalf's work, he never displays the ostentation that must have been in evidence in many homes of the period. Light – here playing around and in the rather fantastic decanter in which a lemon is reflected – was an important problem for Kalf. Light changes form and colour, it both emphasizes and dissolves substance, it creates three-dimensional space and it moulds objects plastically against a dark background. Artists are always confronted by problems of light, and every period tries to find its own solution. In the 17th century with its extrovert lust for life the problem of the scintillating light that emphasizes tangibility occupied many minds. An artist, however, will always transcend tangibility. Despite the obvious identity of the objects in this still life, the dominant quality of the oranges, for example, is their juicy ripeness. The yellow is applied in broad points. Kalf also used this pointed touch to express the glow and the curves of the silver decanter and the gold or gilt standard of the dark, bossed goblet. Here, too, Kalf's delight is evident in scintillating effects and in the subtle and rich pattern of colour. The blue and white china bowl, that could never really stand like this, provides a restful note in contrast with all the glitter. At the same time, though, its pattern of circular, oval, and intersecting lines provides a dynamic touch, as do also the pointed hazelnuts at the left and the open watch with the mauve streamers. The dark background, the solid edge of the table which is, however, intersected several times, and the standard of the glass in the centre serve to achieve balance. An analysis of the composition reveals that all forms and lines, also in the decoration of the objects, were manipulated by Kalf to construct an extremely clever and rhythmical composition.

28. WILLEM KALF
Rotterdam 1619–1693 Amsterdam.

STILL LIFE
canvas 71,5 by 62 cm. A.J.Brandt Sale, 1821.

Few artists have expressed the typical characteristics of children with such skill as Jan Steen. The great masters of art have of course conveyed the essential qualities of a child, even when they were hampered by the demands of formal representation where a royal child was concerned. Seldom, however, do we see children at play, and even less when they are up to mischief. To accomplish this an artist must not only be an excellent craftsman, but he should also have an exceptional visual memory. It is extremely difficult to pose a playing child, certainly when it is in the company of others. Jan Steen had ample opportunity for observing the reactions of children in his own family circle, and he had the rather special gift of being able to relive a situation, as it were. This is admirably illustrated in the 'S. Nicholas Eve'. As always and everywhere, the parents are paying more attention to the small child than to the older ones. One of these, a boy, has received a rod in his shoe as he had been naughty. He will of course get a real present too, and in the background an elderly woman, possibly the grandmother, holds the curtain of the bed and beckons him. The eldest son has good-naturedly taken the baby on his arm and points up the chimney in front of which a child is singing. The thrice repeated groups of three form triangles, a form which appears more than once in the rest of the composition, serving to emphasize tension. Steen has used this device with great sophistication in the dress of the girl, which stands out in a point such as was never actually worn. Without this point, however, the typically hesitatory reaction of going, or not, to her mother to show what she had found in her shoe would disappear. The large angle formed by the fold in the woman's skirt and the sharp point of the girl's dress are indispensable for the expression. The lozenge-shaped 'duvekater' bread, a typical S.Nicholas delicacy, the cakes, fruit, and other objects seemingly littered in the foreground, demonstrate Jan Steen's skill as a still-life painter. He delighted in the commonplace things of everyday life, and he liked to have them in the foreground. This has nothing whatever to do with slovenliness, of which Jan Steen has so frequently been accused.

29. JAN STEEN
Leiden 1626–1679 Leiden.

S. NICHOLAS EVE
canvas 82 by 70,5 cm., signed. From the Cabinet Van Heteren, The Hague, 1809.

Steen had a marked preference for the anecdotal and he also tackled religious themes more than once. He is then in the first place the narrator who transposes the stories from the bible into the context of his own life, and who is not in the least concerned with inspiring people to devotion by his work. Though this 'Adoration' probably never had a place in church or chapel, it is nevertheless imbued with reverence for the new-born Child. Only tradition indicates that the Virgin and the Child are the protagonists. Though the Virgin has been emphasized by the exceptional colouring, Steen paid less attention to the Child than to the boys who are looking on. The rather awe-struck little boy in front of the man with the bagpipes, hardly daring to approach, is very charming. Both colouring and attitude of the Virgin are related via the Utrecht School to the School of Fontainebleau. It is evident that Steen had a thorough knowledge of the work of his predecessors, but he has subordinated it to his own spiritual experience. Though the handling of the Child is rather sketchy and coarse, compositionally Steen certainly gave it due attention. The Virgin's wide robe isolates her from the visitors. Through the effect of its large curve and the slightly raised blanket the Child seems enveloped in her embrace, even though she is not holding it. The eye is led over the diagonally placed manger to the piper. The pipes of his instrument form, in reverse, an angle similar to that made by the approaching visitors with those already watching the Child in quiet devotion. Steen, who was for a short time the pupil of his father-in-law, the landscape painter Jan van Goyen, has conveyed the atmosphere of evening in a wide landscape very beautifully in the small detail of trees and sky. The ox and the ass, so often no more than indispensable attributes, are portrayed with real understanding. Animals quite frequently occupy a rather central position in Steen's compositions and he always arouses interest by his keen observation and the warmth of his treatment. At first glance the ass almost attracts more attention than the Child. Despite Steen's delight in incidental details, despite his expression of a mild sense of humour in the background scene, where S.Joseph seems to be raising his hat to thank a woman for a gift of eggs, in the final analysis he concentrates all attention on the reverence accorded the new-born Child.

30. JAN STEEN
Leiden 1626–1679 Leiden.

THE ADORATION OF THE SHEPHERDS
canvas 53 by 64 cm., signed. Acquired from the A.A. van Sandick Collection, Rotterdam, 1947.

As a subject the woman standing here pouring milk is really quite unimportant. No housewife would care to be photographed, and even less painted, at such a commonplace, trivial occupation. Vermeer has also attached little importance to the physiognomy. The undeniable attraction of the picture does therefore not lie in the woman and her work, but in the artist's handling of the subject. The light colours are remarkable in the first place, in comparison at least with the predominantly dark palette of many 17th-century Dutch painters. Like many of his contemporaries, Vermeer explored the fluctuations of light. Here he tried to suggest the tremulous quality of light by countless small points in both costume and still life. This is a sort of *pointillism* such as was practised by the post-impressionists, the *pointillists* of the 19th century. With these points Vermeer has considerably animated the muted atmosphere; the round objects on the table also serve this purpose. The pose of the hands and the vertical line of the milk can hardly be considered as movement. Movement was always associated with undulating lines, circles, and diagonals, the basic elements indeed of the still life on the table. Unless we were familiar with the objects, we could never recognize or reconstruct most of them with the help of Vermeer's work. To him they primarily represented a compositional medium. The brown wooden footstool, for example, with its brick-red earthen chafing-dish, set obliquely before the lead-grey tiled skirting, is mainly a tension effect that adds considerably to the erect stance of the woman. The clean white headdress has been painted with a fair amount of grey. Vermeer has succeeded exceptionally well in contrasting the various whites and in producing the rich tonal effect of the whitewashed wall. The nails in the wall and the other objects are, simple as they seem, important spatial and colour elements. The most remarkable thing about this picture is the monumental quality that Vermeer has achieved in his rendering of a very ordinary woman of no particular beauty, grace or charm. This has made her the prototype of the quiet busy woman.

31. JOHANNES VERMEER
Delft 1632–1675 Delft.

THE KITCHEN-MAID
canvas 45,5 by 41 cm., circa 1658. Purchased with the aid of the 'Vereeniging' Rembrandt from the Jan Six Collection, Amsterdam, 1908.

32. JOHANNES VERMEER
Delft 1632–1675 Delft.

THE LITTLE STREET
canvas 54,3 by 44 cm., signed, circa 1658. Gift of Sir Henry Deterding, 1921 (acquired from the Jan Six Collection, Amsterdam, 1921).

Johannes Vermeer, who was born in Delft and lived there all his life as far as we know, was not only attracted by quiet figures in an interior, but also by the urban scene. Of the three pictures mentioned in the records, two are known: the large 'View of Delft', now in the Mauritshuis (The Hague) and 'The little Street'. The latter was painted from his own house. Though this picture bears witness to a great love of detail and careful observation, its beauty is not determined by the accurate recording of the houses. What interested Vermeer even more was the transition from one house to the other and the three-dimensional effect. A picturesque interpretation such as this was exceptional at a time when meticulous recording of towns and buildings predominated. Despite a precise treatment of the bricks, Vermeer employed no fussy elaboration of detail; the colour values induced by wind and weather were more important. The windows are painted in untransparent blacks and browns, yet they glow vividly through the effect of the delicate lines and small points. That the right-hand house really is a house with depth and not a mere façade, is achieved not only by the perspective construction at the left, but quite positively by the effect of the figures. They are not significant as personages but as elements of form and colour. The figure in the doorway conveys a three-dimensional effect with the white, while her grey skirt provides a proper balance and a point of yellow on her arm introduces a slight suggestion of action. The children and the woman at the side of the house are also indispensable elements for the depth of the composition. Though the pattern of lines suggests a cobbled street, Vermeer did not draw a single stone. It would only have distracted the attention from what is essential: the wide range of colour in the old house. The numerous horizontals and verticals emphasize tranquillity; they are opposed, however, by diagonal lines and pointed forms in the windows, in the cramp-irons, and notably at the left, where the irregular sequence of the gables contributes greatly to the lively tension. The bluish tint of the leaves against the cottage at the left, where a suspicion of green can still be seen, is caused by yellow sickness, a disease that sometimes occurs in paint. This discolouration, however, hardly detracts from the picture as a whole.

In comparison with 'The Kitchen-Maid' the atmosphere is even more muted in this picture. This is not only due to a change of subject, but quite positively to a change of attitude in the artist. Painters have always been concerned with the problems of light which changes colour and moulds or diffuses form. Vermeer has limited himself in this picture to a few colours and forms. Without painting a window, he has suggested a wide view at the left by the fluid light on the white wall; on the other hand, the browned map, the table and the chairs seem to envelop the woman in intimacy. The woman is patently holding a piece of paper but there is no indication that it is a letter. The angular form of the white suggests that it is paper. Vermeer's primary concern, however, was not the psychological reaction of his models; he needed the white forms for the three-dimensional effect of his composition, just as the bows on the jacket, the shadows of the chair and the knob of the map on the wall have been employed to obtain this effect. But Vermeer is too conscientious an observer not to impart a light expression of concentration to the profile. The sharp nose, the parted lips and the downcast eyes have been handled with great refinement. The blue ribbon that bisects the woman's cheek is a lively diagonal that draws attention to the sensitive profile and at the same time fills in the rather empty plane. Vermeer studied the reciprocal influence of colours. The colour of the skin has been perceptibly infused with the blue of the jacket, which is extremely rich in tonal values. The kind of chair we see here was of course studded with brass nails, but with these points of yellow Vermeer has introduced a lively touch to contrast with the horizontal and vertical forms. The obliquely placed chair and the objects on the table also add to the tension in this blonde and quiet atmosphere.

33. JOHANNES VERMEER
Delft 1632–1675 Delft.

YOUNG WOMAN READING A LETTER
canvas 46,5 by 39 cm., circa 1662/1663.
Bequest to the City of Amsterdam, 1854,
by A. van der Hoop, Amsterdam. On
loan, 1885.

The most striking feature of this picture is its radiant sunniness with its suggestion of a warm summer's day. This is something that was rarely expressed in 17th-century painting. The room is kept cool by the partly closed shutters but the light pours in, tempered through the upper part of the window at the right, scintillating by the open door. Points of light, to a certain extent related to 19th-century *pointillism*, illumines the red-tiled floor which has a wide range of tonal values. The little dark dog catches the light and his pose leads the eye past some branches toward the distance, where a road with high, trimmed poplars and a few houses seems to be indicated beyond a hedge. No more than 'seems' indeed, as it is merely suggested by a few minute forms and touches of colour. Distance is conveyed by a white patch in the sky, by a thin strip of light above the lower door and also by a pencilled line of white separating door and threshold. In this composition, which like 'The Pantry' is constructed on predominantly mathematical lines, a point or a stroke of white is as significant as in many non-figurative 20th-century works. The severe rhythm of squares and rectangles is playfully disrupted by the light and by various circular forms. The brass warming-pan that has been painted with a little yellow draws the attention, which is wandering outdoors at the left, back into the interior, whereas the white pillows in turn lead the glance away from the yellow. The figures had probably been important to the artist from the initial conception of this picture. Though their attitudes have been well observed, the atmosphere of sunny cheerfulness is expressed most intensely by the colours, warm red, white, yellow and blue. The warming-pan is painted mainly in greenish yellow and a little red, the child's skirt in blue-green. The child, the shadow line on the floor, the pinkish plane of light and the shadow on the tiled wall form a triangle that has its apex near the warming-pan. The peaked cap of the woman and the sharp line of her nose are directed downward. The sword that hangs high on the wall has, with the dark shadow, no more than a stabilizing function. This picture is at first glance a charming rendering of an interior, but its beauty is essentially determined by its rhythm and subtle tonal quality.

34. PIETER DE HOOCH
*Rotterdam 1629 – 1683 or later
Amsterdam.*

MATERNAL DUTY
*canvas 52,5 by 61 cm., circa 1660.
Bequest to the City of Amsterdam, 1854,
by A. van der Hoop, Amsterdam. On
loan, 1885.*

Unlike Vermeer, Pieter de Hooch was not born in Delft but he is usually included in the Delft School as his best pictures originated in the period he lived
there (1654 – circa 1662). The light falling into an interior, the beauty of a simple
white wall and of the nuances in brick, all the elements admired in Vermeer are
here. De Hooch liked to use warm colours and his animation is frequently livelier
and less muted than in Vermeer; even so, the figures are not the main theme.
This pantry scene had probably been conceived without the woman and the
child; if we examine it closely we can clearly see that a picture had originally
been hung high on the wall above their heads. De Hooch has painted this out
as it was presumably too heavy an accent. Without the figures, however, the
picture would have been quite appropriate here, and an analysis of the rhythm
then even leads to the conclusion that the composition is a carefully contrived
construction of squares, rectangles, and triangles. This was certainly not done
consciously. De Hooch delighted in the effect of light on colour; he delighted in
form and rhythm; he did not aim to give a recording of wall, floor, and windows.
It is only since the advent of photography, which today more than satisfies the
desire for 'looking at pictures', that artists can dispense with anything that resem-
bles a recording; the more so, now science teaches us that matter is energy.
Though he had a thorough knowledge of perspective, as was to be expected in
the 17th century, De Hooch has in fact suggested three-dimensional space through
the effect of the light playing on the white, untransparent cellar-window and by
the white wall, that can be seen through the open window, with its suggestion
of an alley i.e. of distance. The pure, simple forms and the taut composition are
essentially the same elements that in the 20th century led Mondrian to his se-
verely constructed compositions. By then, however, it had become a more con-
scious process.

35. PIETER DE HOOCH
Rotterdam 1629–1685 or later
Amsterdam.

THE PANTRY
canvas 65 by 60,5 cm., signed, circa
1658. Acquired from the collection of
Mrs. Hogguer, Amsterdam.

The little daughter of the Reverend van der Schalcke was presumably painted about 1644 by Ter Borch at the same time as her parents. He seldom had the opportunity for painting such a colourful portrait. It is very difficult for an artist to convey the liveliness of a small child, especially when movement is hampered by the costume. The parents presumably desired a formal portrait in the first instance. Ter Borch's meticulous, though never fussy, technique and his careful observation of the child, however, make this an extremely attractive little portrait. There are delicate nuances in the white which has been beautifully enlivened by the pink carnation, the red ribbons and gold chain. The wicker-basket with its dark-green bands is an indispensable element in achieving a lively pose, both in the effect of its oval form and its soft yellow colour. The hands, a small oblique plane behind the right arm, and the circular skirt combine to convey an impression of curbed movement. Straight fair hair hangs down under the close-fitting cap; the large brown eyes redeem the rather old expression of the sharp little face. The child is obviously standing despite the fact that her legs are not indicated and her skirt does not touch the ground. Ter Borch has realized this by a fine play of line and form, in which the vertical plane of the pinafore emphasizes the standing attitude with a few deep shadows. In contrast with Jan Steen, who portrayed people and especially children in action, Ter Borch was a master of restrained movement and of the portrait which afforded him the opportunity for expressing his delight in a quiet and delicate play of colour. As the son of an artist he was able to develop his talent early. He travelled extensively, visiting England, Italy and Spain, and though he undoubtedly studied the work of other artists closely, he retained his individuality. We cannot escape the impression, however, that on his travels he may have seen work by Velázquez, who had so brilliantly portrayed the infantas in their wide costumes. Though such work may have influenced him in the composition of Helena van der Schalcke's portrait, he has done no more than show this simple little girl, who was the pride of her parents, in her own small world, a rather saucy and inquisitive, but also rather shy, child. Ter Borch, who had an extensive knowledge of art, displayed wisdom and self-knowledge in not exceeding the bounds of his extremely sensitive but limited talent.

36. GERARD TER BORCH
Zwolle 1617–1681 Deventer.

HELENA VAN DER SCHALCKE
as a Child
*panel 34 by 28,5 cm., circa 1644.
Purchased in Amsterdam with aid of
the 'Vereeniging Rembrandt', 1898.*

Many artists who enjoyed a great reputation in their own time, and even long after, have lost much of their fame in the 20th century. We have a different approach to art, and the anecdotal element, which brought renown to many 17th-century artists, only has significance for us as a source of information on morals and customs. Philips Wouwerman, for example, whose work was well represented in many great 18th-century collections is now primarily of art-historical interest. Even so, we can still admire important pictorial qualities in much of his work. It is mainly his more restrained compositions that are still generally appreciated, where he devotes himself entirely to his love of horses that appear in an endless variety in his pictures, and where he shows himself as an able colourist. The handling of colour is skilfully accomplished in this simple composition of a white horse standing on a dune. Living in Haarlem, Wouwerman knew this landscape well and he frequently painted horses walking in the yellowish grey sand, often near a pool. Here he was chiefly concerned with the range of tones in the white coat and the grey mane and tail. The warm red saddle is a fine colour effect, but also equally important as a formal element that serves to diminish the air of fatigue of the animal. The saddle provides a logical break in the long line of the back, and the slightly upward curves form an excellent contrast with the many downward verticals. The pollard willow at the left restricts the composition and at the same time acts as a spatial effect with the upward curving branches. The cloudy sky in fluent greyish white tones leads the attention toward the distance, and is also a tonal background for the horse. The painter follows the conventional landscape scheme. The greyish half figure at the right is merely an instrument to achieve a fluent transition to the horizon. The boy, too, who is holding the horse is only significant as form and colour. Though Wouwerman was presumably inspired by a horse he knew well, he has not produced an actual portrait. The horse is not posed as in many equestrian portraits or other pictures with horses; its natural attitude seems to have been captured instantaneously. Herein also lies the charm of Wouwerman's picture.

37. PHILIPS WOUWERMAN
Haarlem 1619–1668 Haarlem.

THE WHITE HORSE
panel 43,5 by 38 cm., signed. Acquired with the aid of the 'Vereeniging Rembrandt', 1894.

Considering the geographical and economic circumstances of the Netherlands, it is natural that the inhabitants should show an interest in representations of the sea. This is not manifested, however, in an uninterrupted series of marine paintings in Dutch art, as we would expect. On the contrary, we find that the painters only sporadically displayed an interest in the sea and water. The vastness, infinity and mystery of the sea, that fetches and carries, enriches and destroys, the perpetual motion and the ever-changing colours, these were hardly pondered concepts in an era when representation of the concrete predominated. We speak of 17th-century sea painters, though it would in most cases be more correct to call them 'portrayers of ships'. In the work of Willem van de Velde the Younger the portrayal of ships is undoubtedly predominant, but there is an unmistakable atmosphere in many of his pictures. Clouds and water do not only serve as a background for the vessels, though the wide range of grey tones is of course very effective as a contrast for the white or yellow sails. Here he has added another white cloud as an extra touch, the smoke of the fired shot. This is primarily a colour and light effect. The vibration of the ship has not been indicated; everything is mirror-smooth and calm. A breeze slightly ruffles the water and plays through the rigging. With a beautifully firm hand Van de Velde drew flapping riggings like these in calligraphic lines. He undoubtedly owed his love of line to his father, whose pen drawings on panel and canvas betray his skilled draughtsmanship. His second teacher, the sea painter Simon de Vlieger, was more a colourist. In this picture Van de Velde is less concerned with the representation of a specific vessel than with the composition as a whole. Horizontal lines emphasize heaviness, whereas the many diagonals running in different directions and the tall mast suggest motion. The hanging sails with the heavy shadows are more than a technical indication that the ship is lying still. The restful effect of horizontal lines is an important element in the composition. Van de Velde has not yet realized a suggestion of motion in the straining backs of the rowers; he accomplished this to a certain extent in the three gulls in the foreground. Together with the shadow of the ship they introduce a three-dimensional effect into the composition, that has, amazingly, not been accomplished by sea and sky.

38. WILLEM VAN DE VELDE, THE YOUNGER
Leiden 1633–1707 London.

THE CANNON SHOT
canvas 78,5 by 67 cm., signed. Bequest to the City of Amsterdam, 1854, by A. van der Hoop, Amsterdam. On loan in the Rijksmuseum since 1885.

In the 17th century Holland was extremely rich in painters who still rank among the internationally important artists, some of them even among the giants of all time. The last decades of the century, however, were marked by complacency and smugness, artistically and commercially. The patrons who commissioned portraits were hardly inspiring men. Genre motifs, the domestic scenes so dear to the heart of the ordinary man, were repeated in endless variations. One of the very few to transcend the drab superficiality and fussy detail was Cornelis Troost. He has left several excellent portraits and a series of pastels wittily illustrating popular plays. The performing of music was evidently a popular pastime in the 18th century. In 17th-century paintings, in fact, people were already frequently depicted with musical instruments. Seldom, however, was there any attempt to translate the essence of music or rhythm into line and colour. It was only with Cubism in this century that musical rhythm and tension became of primary importance. Troost's treatment of the cello, which he has placed against a chair with a purple cushion, is mainly pictorial, with high-lights and a reddish glow in the brown surface. There is not the slightest indication that the man has just been playing or is about to do so. For, though the open book does indeed reveal a music-score, the coat-of-arms on the opposite page is more significant and the emphasis here is really on the colour and spatial effect. The man, moreover, is holding a drawing in his hand, and this again is essentially a rhythmical and colour element. Together with celestial globe and half-open book-case, these are indications of the versatile cultural interests of this hitherto unknown man. The various greys in wig, costume, and stockings have been handled in a lively manner, and Troost has made the most of the colour effect provided by the white powder-stain on the shoulder. The pale blue lining of coat and waist-coat, the white jabot and cuffs are indispensable light tones in the rather dark composition. The red rug with a rather pointed, bluish green pattern provides a lively basis. Wigs and tight-fitting costumes were very characteristic fashion elements in the first half of the 18th century. They were supposedly meant to emphasize a much desired often rather sham, dignity. Cornelis Troost has more than once hinted that he saw through the pretense. And if he never actually ridiculed it, he certainly allowed himself a sly smile.

39. CORNELIS TROOST
Amsterdam 1697–1750 Amsterdam.

PORTRAIT OF A MUSIC LOVER
panel of oak, 72 × 57 cm; signed on the globe: 'C. Troost. 1736'. Purchased from Messrs. Speelman, London, 1958.

This townscape is remarkable for its restraint and atmosphere, and all the more so when we realize that it had been painted in 1809 by a young man of twenty-nine. Van Troostwijk gives evidence of a profound observation of nature and an extraordinary sense of rhythm in his pattern of forms and lines, but he does not indulge in romanticism or laboured narrative. This composition shows him as well ahead of his time. Architectural recording has been reduced to a minimum. Forms dissolve in the hazy atmosphere that precedes a thaw. Even the Wester-toren in the background is no more than a vague outline. It is also, however, an elongated form, a vertical line which contributes to the stability and the height of the composition together with other elements such as the chimney-stacks, the street-lantern, and the railings. The long stretch of wall, sharply outlined by a frieze of soft snow, is a stable horizontal element. The soft quality is suggested by the break in the snow above the water-gate and by the undulating line at the Raampoort. Fluent lines and circular touches also indicate the snow at the water's edge. Linear elements alternate with circular, which are here introduced in the two archways, in the drawbridge, and in the bisected wheel of the wagon, demonstrating the artist's concentration on his compositional rhythm. The fig-ures have no significance at all as individuals, only as elements of form and colour. The red and white of the woman accentuate the depth of the archway. The horse and the man on the bridge relieve the linear severity. These houses and both the archways have long since vanished. Given the practically geometrical compo-sition, it remains an open question whether the scene has been described with topographical accuracy. In addition to the design, the tonal values have great importance. There is a wide range of whites and greys, with dark tones to coun-teract vagueness. The red roofs and the red skirt provide a bright, but not obtru-sive accent. Records show that Wouter van Troostwijk's talent had met with immediate recognition. A predilection for landscape and cattle is evident in the comparatively little that has survived of his work. Studies of figures and a self portrait, painted with a relatively broad brush, justify the supposition that, had he lived, he might have opened new perspectives in what had become the tradi-tional Dutch style in the late 18th and early 19th century.

40. WOUTER JOANNES
VAN TROOSTWIJK
Amsterdam 1782–1810 Amsterdam.

THE 'RAAMPOORTJE' AT AMSTERDAM
canvas, 57 × 48 cm; signed and dated right, on the bank: 'w.j. van Troost-wijk 1809'. On loan since 1902.

When Matthijs Maris painted this souvenir of Amsterdam in Paris in 1871, relying on his memory and possibly on an earlier sketch or a photograph, it could not have been his intention to evoke an actual scene. Attempts have been made to identify the locality, but the main interest does not of course lie in the subject but in its representation: the rather tight composition of the compact masses of tall houses, with the pale light of the sky, however, counteracting any sense of confinement. A matted dark red in one or two roofs and a touch of greyish blue in a door and in a low building are the strongest colours amid the grey, dirty white, and brown tones. The woman at the helm of the barge which is squeezing through the lock has been introduced because of her white cap, not because of her significance as a person. This minute white touch has a strong spatial effect, and so has the man in black who is leaning on the railing. A vaguely indicated white horse and a few other figures are necessary colour and formal elements. The massive horizontals and verticals of the drawbridge, which is joined by dark diagonals to the ground, form an extremely important compositional device. They emphasize the spaciousness and the almost monumental aspect of the scene. Maris will certainly have known drawbridges in his native city The Hague, but amid the tall houses and warehouses on the canals of Amsterdam their impact would have been much more formidable. He must have been fascinated on a visit to Amsterdam by the peculiar atmosphere of the city, which he has recaptured in a way that recalls it vividly to the mind of anyone who has ever wandered through the old town. The lock, lock-keeper's house, high walled sides of the canal, railings, and bridge have been described with more or less accuracy. The rest, drained of all detail, has been suggested in a for the time extremely modern manner. Matthijs Maris's sojourn in Paris from 1867 to 1872 coincided with the early years of Impressionism, which particularly influenced his two-year older brother Jacob who also worked in Paris. Monet was their contemporary, and it is conceivable that, apart from the Barbizon painters, they had become acquainted with the revolutionary Impressionist theories of light and colour. Matthijs Maris is less known, however, for the impressionistic tendencies in some of his earlier work than for the shadowy, spectral figures and the dreamlike quality inherent in later work.

41. MATTHIJS MARIS
The Hague 1839–1917 London.

'SOUVENIR D'AMSTERDAM'
panel of mahogany, 46 × 35 cm; signed with initials and dated lower left: 'M. M. 71'. Collection W.J. van Randwijck. Presented by the heirs, The Hague, 1914.

Artists have recorded their impressions of the urban scene in countless paintings which were usually architectural descriptions, with human figures serving as staffage. Only in rare instances did they realize an atmosphere that was truly evocative of the mood of a town. Breitner, a native of Rotterdam, did this for Amsterdam in his interpretation of the brisk liveliness, and at the same time the placid calm, that is still so typical of the city. The situation may have altered in details but the tall, narrow houses with their suggestion of lively activity behind the windows, even though not a soul is to be seen, still border the canals. The sailing-boats may have vanished but the dark barges with their gaily painted bands are still there, and the open spire of the Oude Kerk (Old Church) still towers over the houses of the Damrak. Breitner was not interested in an exact architectural recording but in the greyish brown forms as such seen against the heavily clouded sky, where an impression of movement and expanse is suggested by the use of a rich scala of greys and whites. Breitner is an exceptional impressionist. Only very few artists have been able to lay such a richness of tone in dark, heavy colours. Never, even when he paints rain-drenched streets, is the atmosphere depressed. The window-articulation in the row of houses here provides an extremely varied rhythmical pattern, and the wide range of white tones, reminiscent of curtains, are primarily elements of light and life. The tall masts accentuate the high spire. The pointed forms of mast-heads, the diagonals of ropes, sails, and gables, the circular forms of vats and of a wheel contribute to the animation of the scene together with the vivid red in a child in the foreground, the blue tones in boats and gables, and the touches of yellow. Breitner's technical mastery, notably his draughtsmanship, is clearly perceptible in his work. Though he had transcended his academic training, he constantly needed to consider the nature of things. More than anything else, however, his main concern has become the problem of light which effects changes in colour and imparts a certain buoyancy to houses, ships, and people. This has enabled him to convey an impression of life, even when people are not, or hardly suggested. A close and detailed study of a picture like this reveals to what extent Impressionism anticipated non-figurative 20th-century art.

42. GEORGE HENDRIK BREITNER
Rotterdam 1857–1923 Amsterdam.

THE 'DAMRAK' IN AMSTERDAM
canvas 100 × 150 cm; signed lower left: 'G.H.Breitner'. – Bequest A. van Wezel, Amsterdam, 1922.

It is highly improbable that Hendrik Vroom, who is known as a very accurate painter of shipping, could have sketched his preparatory drawings on the scene of this naval action in which the Dutch defeated the Spanish fleet. On his many voyages, however, he must have had ample opportunity to study ships and he had undoubtedly experienced piracies, fighting at sea, and storms. Despite its apparent gruesome realism, this painting actually has great compositional and colouristic sophistication and is anything but naturalistic. In no other of the countless naval battles recorded in 17th-century art has suspense been so strongly suggested as it is here. All external factors have been subordinated to this element. The billowing sails form taut arcs and ovals. As far as Vroom is concerned, it is quite irrelevant that a torn sail will not fill and that the rigging of a broken mast is apt to become a tangled mess. He has suggested the suspense at the moment of explosion with an extremely skilful manipulation of line. The two wooden ships are obviously doomed to perish in the raging fire which Vroom has handled, however, as a fine colour effect rather than a destructive element. The large Spanish vessel is disintegrating; her masts, still connected by the halyards, are coming down in opposite directions; the long pennant floats upward, focussing the attention on the curved line, partially formed by the bodies and objects hurtling through the air, which extends to the Dutch vessel. Here the movement is less violent, but masts and tackle form a fine dynamic pattern and the curves of her sails, which have caught fire from the blazing Spanish vessel, form a structural unity with the sails of the latter. Many dramatic events are evidently taking place, yet the numerous figures have essentially no more than narrative significance. Vroom expresses no emotional involvement with, and certainly no denunciation of the catastrophic event and the concomitant human suffering. He has quite unintentionally constructed a very tense, highly charged composition with the aid of recognizable objects, but in essence with line, form, and colour. The sails of the surrounding ships help to emphasize the expression of movement but the rippling surface of the sea is merely a base for the ships. No marine painter seems to have seriously considered the vital importance of wind and weather in naval warfare. Vroom has given some attention, however, to the waves in the foreground, notably in the colour. Many paintings in the Department of Netherlands History are of great documentary interest; this work of Vroom's excels in aesthetical qualities.

43. HENDRIK CORNELISZ(OON) VROOM
Haarlem 1562/63–1640 Haarlem.

THE BATTLE OF GIBRALTAR
25th April 1607. Won by the Dutch under command of Admiral Jacob van Heemskerck. Canvas, 137,5×188 cm; acquired at the sale Fr. Muller & Co., Amsterdam, 1905.

Posthumous fame has come to many people by virtue of the artists who had painted their portraits. This is certainly the case with the wives of artists, whose only claim to renown lies in the fact that they had once, maybe more than once, inspired their husbands. Women had presumably served as models for the saints and allegorical figures of their husbands even when in the concept of a period the individual was hardly important enough to be the subject of a portrait. This is usually assumed when a certain, more or less idealized figure is repeated in an *œuvre*. Margaretha van Eyck, wife of the Flemish painter Jan van Eyck, is one of the first known artists' wives. In the 16th and 17th century there appeared a whole series, among them Isabella Brandt and Helena Fourment, Saskia van Uylenburgh and Hendrickje Stoffels, who had shared the lives of Rubens and Rembrandt and acquired international fame. Both men had married a much younger woman after the death of the first wife. Here, however, all resemblance stops. The very distinct personalities of Rubens and Rembrandt bore the unmistakable imprint of their Flemish and Dutch origin, they were a generation apart in age, and their cultural background was completely different. We can only get an inkling of Rubens's great artistry from the two portraits and a sketch in oils for a large altarpiece of the Procession to Calvary with which he is represented in the Rijksmuseum. As a man of the world, diplomat and painter, Rubens repeatedly emphasized glamour and elegance. Helena Fourment wears the lavish jewellery, which was primarily painted for its lustrous quality, with great style. The warm glow of her flesh under the white pearls has been realized by a liberal use of red in the shadows. The cool white silk is set off by the gold and a red accent has been applied in some of the gems. Helena Fourment frequently posed for Rubens. She must have appeared to the mature man as the embodiment of all that young and rich life that flourished anew, also in Antwerp where he lived and worked, in the revival at the end of the eighty-years war with which he must have been closely involved as a diplomat. Rubens was an adherent of the religious principles of the Counter-Reformation. He fully accepted life in all its aspects and the period which began with his second marriage in 1630 was extremely productive. This portrait of Helena Fourment is a version of a detail of the full-length work (1630/31), now in the Old Pinakothek in Munich.

44. SIR PETRUS PAULUS RUBENS
Siegen (Westphalia) 1577–1640 Antwerp.

HELENA FOURMENT (1614–1673)
Second wife of the artist, in wedding dress. Panel of oak, 75 × 56 cm. Free repetition of a part of the full-length portrait painted in 1630/31, in the Old Pinakothek in Munich. Bequest to the City of Amsterdam, 1854. On loan, since 1885, in the Rijksmuseum.

The numerous flower-paintings executed in the 17th century in North and South Netherlands may lead to the conclusion that flowers were very much in evidence in 17th-century homes, but this is presumably a too modern interpretation. Only in isolated cases were the frequently massive arrangements painted entirely from nature. The pictures are mostly colour compositions in which flowers of different seasons are combined. Tulips, which derived from Turkey and were introduced into the Low Countries in the 16th century, repeatedly come in for a great deal of attention. The desire for a "portrait" of the then exotic and costly flower should perhaps be seen in relation to the notorious, in many instances disastrous, tulip trade in the 17th century. Only rarely, however, does the tulip appear by itself. The work of Jan Brueghel demonstrates an approach that is to a certain extent akin to that of the 15th-century artist who explored nature in great detail, with evident pleasure in the recording of individual flowers and plants which had till then merely been elements in a general suggestion of nature. With the advent of the Renaissance the knowledge of exterior qualities had become an aim in itself. This knowledge was certainly important to Jan Brueghel, but the appeal of colour was stronger still. He has taken no trouble to produce a convincing arrangement of the flowers in the wooden tub; the lengths of the stems are quite wrong, and all these flowers could not possibly fit into the receptacle; heavy flowers appear at the top and flowers with slender stalks, giving an impression of lightness, are just pushed in anywhere. We only realize this, however, after a close scrutiny. The first impression is one of joyfulness, of *joie-de-vivre*, even though sun and light and space have been left out of the picture. The dark background emphasizes the decorative effect which may make this and similar work too elaborate for modern taste. It is evident that Jan Brueghel knew the various flowers well and that he had tried to reproduce their typical charateristics. Insects and butterflies create a natural impression and demonstrate Brueghel's knowledge of animal life which is expressed in a meticulous recording. Naturalistic description, however, is never carried to extremes. This is illustrated, for example, in his handling of the peony where, with no indication of individual petals he has given priority to colour. Considered purely as a colouristic composition, this work demonstrates Brueghel's concern in achieving an equilibrium between the dynamic yellows, the warm reds, the delicate whites and pinks, the blues and quiet greens.

45. JAN BRUEGHEL THE ELDER
called 'Velvet Brueghel' or 'Flower Brueghel'. Brussels 1568–1625 Antwerp.

LARGE FLOWER-PIECE
panel of oak, 113 × 86 cm. Replica after a piece in the Old Pinakothek in Munich. Gift of Mr. and Mrs. Kessler-Hülsmann, 1940.

The portrait of the carpenter and architect Francesco Giamberti who died in 1480 was not painted from life, though the vital head and the elaboration of detail suggest that the artist must have known the man personally. Scrupulous recording like this of wrinkles, veins, and stubble on the chin occurred frequently in 15th-century Flemish art. The situation of a figure against a landscape background in which people and buildings have been set down with evident pleasure is equally illustrative of Flemish influence. This should only be seen, however, as a source of inspiration. Piero di Cosimo was undoubtedly acquainted with Italian medal-portraits, but here again he did not imitate. The head is placed in profile while the sturdy figure shows a decided forward torsion. Very remarkable is the spirited expression in the head, with the fallen-in mouth and the wrinkles nevertheless emphasizing age. The upward sweep of the hair in the neck, the grey hairs curling lightly against the strange red cap with the undulating brim, and even the curiously shaped ear soften the lines of contour and tight-lipped mouth. The eyebrows which contribute to the lively expression are suggested by a few thin, incisive strokes. The sheet of music is a rather unexpected attribute of a carpenter-architect. Francesco Giamberti may have been an amateur musician, and the organ outside the church at the right may likewise be an allusion to this fact. There has been no evidence thus far that a definite piece of music is referred to here. As a formal element, however, the lozenge-shaped notes on the folded white paper help to express the spiritual intensity of the man. In contrast with this is the fluent curved line of the shirt. This extremely personal portrait has a companion picture in the no less personal portrait of the son, the architect Giuliano da San Gallo, which, judging by the rather more modern style, must have originated about ten tears later. Giorgio Vasari, the biographer of many artists, had seen both these portraits in the mid-16th century at Giamberti's grandson Francesco da San Gallo.It is still a mystery how the portraits came to be in England, where they were in the collection of William III, king of England and stadtholder of the Netherlands. Later they came to Holland by inheritance. The names of the artist and his sitters had, however, been buried in oblivion and the portraits were at various times ascribed to Holbein and Dürer. There was evidently never any doubt about their quality. It was only in the late 19th century that Piero di Cosimo was recognized as the author.

46. PIERO DI COSIMO called Piero di Lorenzo. *Florence 1462–1521 Florence.*

FRANCESCO GIAMBERTI (1405–1480) *A joiner, father of Giuliano da San Gallo. Panel of poplar-wood, 47,5 × 33,5 cm. Painted about 1505 after the death of the sitter. Lent by the Mauritshuis, The Hague, 1948.*

To appreciate Goya's work to the full one must go to Madrid. In the Netherlands his etchings are well represented but his paintings are rare. Goya painted this portrait of a fifty-eight-year old judge late in his life but he was still as vital and caustic as in earlier work. As court painter he had become proficient in conveying sophisticated elegance. He was, however, too keen an observer and too strong a personality to flatter his subjects. In his suggestion of foolish vanity he was, indeed, often pitiless. That he had not mellowed with age is demonstrated in this portrait of an undeniably intelligent man. Standing very aloof, both hands in his pockets, the elbows at a sharp angle, the bearing of the man is expressive of his character. Compositionally it also conveys a suggestion of depth, as do the white points of the shirt-collar. The right half of the face is less passionate than the left. This is confirmed by the gently curving lines of coat, waistcoat, and shirt, which form a fine colour pattern in black, red, and white. The white point of the collar on the left shoulder, a form which is repeated in the elbow, has, however, been strongly emphasized ... The fleshy roundness of the head is accentuated by the ear and the black curls but neutralized by the V-shaped neck-line. Transcending material expression in as far as that was possible at the time, Goya demonstrates a superb technical mastery in this portrait. He was easily one of the greatest painters of the world in the late 18th and early 19th century, if not the greatest. He also gives evidence of a mentality which, under influence of his origin and personality, represents an alien element in the collection of the Rijksmuseum. As a Spaniard, his mental attitude differed in many respects from that of other nationalities. Cynicism coupled with a certain love of cruelty is a quality Goya had never quite conquered, though he had himself been subjected to indignity and suffering. It is true that most of his models were in a different social class than the Dutch *burghers*, but the emotional approach of an artist such as Frans Hals, for instance, was also completely different. Hals was a no less keen observer of human frailty than Goya, nor was his ridicule exactly mild, but the attitude of reserve which characterizes many of his later portraits is one that suggests the *Einmaligkeit* of the individual. With Goya the reserve suggests arrogance, and man in his concept is apparently not an in the final analysis fathomless mystery.

47. FRANCISCO JOSÉ DE GOYA Y LUCIENTES
Fuentetodos near Saragossa 1746–1828 Bordeaux.

DON RAMÓN SATUE (1765–1824)
Alcalde de Corte (i.e. judge in the palace quarter of Madrid). Canvas, 107 × 83,5 cm; signed and dated lower left: 'D. Ramon Satue, Alcalde de Corte, Pr. Goya 1823'. Purchased with aid of members of the 'Vereeniging Rembrandt', 1922.

The pastel artist Liotard is well represented in the Rijksmuseum, notably with a series of portraits of polite 18th-century society. They give an illuminating chronicle of that dashing and elegant era in which Liotard himself must have cut a rather dashing figure. When he visited Turkey, travelling there from Italy, he was completely fascinated by the exotic life he encountered in that country. Such was his enchantment that he decided to live like a Turk himself, even appearing at Maria Theresia's court in Vienna in Turkish costume and wearing a long beard. She does not seem to have taken exception to this rather unconventional behaviour as she frequently commissioned him to work for her. Her portrait and portraits of several of her children are known to us. Liotard did not probe very deeply into the personality of his sitters and yet he was able to convey a quite convincing impression of the people he had met on his extensive travels. After his marriage in 1756, he settled in his native city Geneva. The date of this landscape is not known but it certainly belongs to his later period. It is a rather curious composition in which the artist, unexpectedly modest in a corner, is looking over a high wall at the wide prospect. His position here is not the vantage-point from which he had constructed his landscape. Topographically he has probably given a fairly accurate recording. The emphasis on the horizontal lines, the strong vertical accent of the window-frame at the right, the angle of the wall which is repeated in the meadow and the fields in the central plane, indicate that he must have been consciously aware of the constructive process of this for him unusual subject. White effects were introduced elsewhere to balance the snow-capped mountains in the distance. Architectural severity is relieved by the trees, the broken ground, the arched hedge, and the vines. The self portrait is primarily a colourful accent. The vivid red and the blue introduce a warm and lively note whereas the white collar and the placing of the figure contribute to the spatial expression. The element of vanity which had been evident in several other portraits of himself has been eliminated here. He may have been aware of his own insignificance in the face of nature. This is not, however, in any sense a great landscape. His handling of the mountains demonstrates that Liotard had not recognized the qualities of primeval change and growth in nature. Quite in accordance with the mood of his time, he responded in the first instance to the charming and the delightful which has not developed, however, into cloying romanticism or mere scenography.

48. JEAN-ETIENNE LIOTARD
Geneva 1702–1789 Geneva.

LANDSCAPE NEAR GENEVA
View from Liotard's studio. Left, the painter himself. Pastel on parchment, 45 × 58 cm. At the back the inscription: 'Vue de Genève du Cabinet peinte par Liotard'. Gift of Mrs. Tilanus née Liotard, 1885.

INDEX